FORMED BY THE WORD

TRAINING ADVENTIST LEADERS FOR FAITHFUL STUDY AND PREACHING

MICHAEL A. REAHL

Published by
Advent Awareness Publishing & Media
An imprint of Advent Awareness Ministries LLC
Alaska, United States

All Scripture quotations are taken from the English Standard Version (ESV), unless otherwise noted.

Printed in the United States of America.

Dedication

*To the elders, lay leaders, and faithful servants of
the church who open the*

*Word of God week after week often with little recognition but
with deep love for Christ and His people.*

May you be formed by the Word you teach.

Table of Contents

Preface
Why This Book Exists

The Seventh day Adventist Church has always depended on shared leadership. From its earliest days, the movement advanced not because of abundance, but because of faithfulness. Believers gathered in homes, schoolhouses, and small congregations. They studied Scripture together, prayed together, and spoke from conviction shaped by the Word of God. Ministry was not centralized in a few professionals. It was carried by a people.

In many places today, especially in Alaska and other rural or under resourced regions, that reality remains. While shaped by Alaska's unique challenges, these principles equip elders everywhere pastors rotate, resources are scarce, or lay leaders carry preaching loads. Distance is not theoretical. Congregations are separated by geography, weather, limited transportation, and rotating pastoral presence. Elders and lay leaders often carry responsibility for preaching, teaching, visitation, and spiritual care not as an exception, but as a regular calling.

This book exists because that calling deserves preparation.

Too often, faithful elders are asked to serve without being equipped. They are willing, sincere, and committed to the church, yet left to rely on borrowed sermons, rushed preparation, or their own uncertainty. Over time, this creates discouragement. Some speak without confidence. Others stop speaking altogether. The problem is not lack of devotion. It is lack of formation.

The Adventist movement has never believed that the solution to this challenge is performance. It has believed in training. Ellen G White's counsel that every church should be a training school for Christian workers was not idealistic theory.[1] It was practical instruction rooted in lived church life. Training was understood not as professionalization, but as faithfulness. It was meant to form character, habits, and understanding long before public speaking ever took place.

This book is written in conversation with the established guidance of the Seventh day Adventist Church and is intended to support, not replace, the responsibilities entrusted to local elders and lay leaders. It assumes the

---

1 Ellen G. White, *The Ministry of Healing* (Mountain View, CA: Pacific Press Publishing Association, 1905), 149.2.

standards and order outlined by the Church and seeks to strengthen those who serve within them.

This book was written for elders and lay leaders who serve where resources are limited but responsibility is great. It was written for churches where pastors may rotate or cover multiple congregations. It was written for those who open Scripture before others and feel the weight of that trust. It assumes that readers are intelligent, sincere, and willing to learn, even when time is short and conditions are demanding.

The purpose of this book is not to make experts, but to form servants. It does not offer shortcuts. It does not promise quick results. It invites leaders to slow down, to study carefully, to pray consistently, and to allow Scripture to shape them before they attempt to shape others.

In the pages that follow, Adventist identity, history, and mission are treated as foundational, not optional. Bible study is presented as a spiritual discipline before it is a teaching task. Sermon foundations are offered as tools of stewardship, not products to be consumed. Local context, culture, and lived experience are honored, because faithful preaching is always incarnational.

Throughout this book, readers will encounter the voices and experiences of early Adventist leaders whose own words reveal how careful Bible study shaped conviction before public proclamation. The aim is not only to provide material for teaching, but to cultivate habits of patient reading, thoughtful observation, and reverent listening that can be carried into every passage of Scripture.

This work is offered with humility and hope. It is not meant to replace pastoral leadership, formal education, or the guidance of the Holy Spirit. It is meant to walk alongside those who have been called to serve, often quietly and consistently, in places where faithfulness matters more than visibility.

If this book helps one elder approach Scripture with greater care, one lay leader prepare with greater confidence, or one congregation be strengthened through faithful teaching, it will have served its purpose.

Introduction
A People of the Word in a Place of Distance

The Seventh day Adventist Church has always understood itself to be a people shaped by Scripture. Our identity, message, and mission did not arise from cultural influence or institutional power, but from sustained engagement with the Word of God. From the beginning, Adventists believed that Scripture was not only authoritative, but accessible. Ordinary believers were expected to read it, wrestle with it, and share what they understood with humility and conviction.

That conviction becomes especially significant in places where distance shapes daily life. In rural, remote, and under resourced contexts, preaching and teaching are not always supported by proximity to seminaries, libraries, or consistent pastoral presence. Yet the need for faithful instruction remains. In such places, the local church does not wait for ideal conditions. It depends on elders and lay leaders who are willing to open the Bible before others and speak carefully in the name of Christ.

This book is written for that reality.

It is written with the conviction that careful Bible study, practiced patiently and shared humbly, has always been the foundation of Adventist life and witness.

The principles described in this book are not abstract. They have been lived out quietly and faithfully by elders and lay leaders who have carried the work of the church in places where consistency, patience, and presence matter more than visibility.

Elder Vecous Waite entered lay ministry in 1991 in Jamaica, serving as head elder in the local church. Alongside him, Loretta Waite served in family life ministry and as head deaconess. Their ministry was rooted in Scripture, personal visitation, and steady community engagement rather than programs or performance. At Seaview Gardens Seventh day Adventist Church, a congregation of approximately fifty members grew to more than two hundred through sustained lay leadership and faithful outreach.

That same spirit of ministry was later carried into rural Alaska. For more than eight years, Elder Waite and Loretta Waite have labored in communities such as Bethel, AK and now Togiak, AK where the realities of distance, weather, and limited resources shape daily church life. In places where congregations once gathered only a handful of members, consistent attendance has grown over time through relational ministry, practical service, and the steady opening of Scripture.

What is most instructive about their ministry is not numerical growth alone, but the method. They did not wait for ideal conditions or rely on constant pastoral presence. They studied the Word carefully, prayed consistently, visited faithfully, and allowed Scripture to shape both their lives and their leadership. Their example reflects the same study-first, proclamation-second pattern seen among early Adventist leaders who allowed understanding to mature through sustained engagement with Scripture.

Adventist preaching has never belonged exclusively to professional clergy. It has always been communal, rooted in shared study, prayer, and accountability. Elders were not simply administrators. They were spiritual leaders entrusted with the care of souls and the responsibility of teaching. That trust has not diminished with time. If anything, it has grown heavier in contexts where leadership must be shared and preparation must be intentional.

Throughout this book, historical reflection, Scripture study, and practical guidance are intentionally woven together. Pioneer voices, careful reading practices, and modest use of biblical study tools are included not to overwhelm, but to train readers to approach the Word with greater attentiveness and confidence.

The chapters that follow are designed to form readers before they instruct them. Identity comes before method. Scripture comes before sermons. Faithfulness comes before visibility. The goal is not to produce speakers, but servants shaped by the Word.

Purpose of This Book

This is not a book of sermon manuscripts. It is not a guide for performance, and it is not a substitute for personal Bible study or the work of the Holy Spirit. This book exists for a different purpose.

It is a training reference designed to help elders and lay leaders learn how to handle Scripture faithfully, confidently, and in a Christ-centered way. Each outline models sound biblical practice while remaining simple and flexible enough to be used in a variety of settings, including Sabbath School, divine worship, vespers, small groups, or home Bible studies.

The aim of this book is not polished delivery or rhetorical skill. The aim is faithful understanding. Before words are spoken publicly, Scripture must be understood carefully and received personally. This book seeks to cultivate that posture.

How to Use This Book

This book is a training companion for elders and lay leaders called to open Scripture before others. It is **not** a collection of sermons, a source of ready scripts, or a shortcut for preparation. Instead, it offers a consistent pattern to help you study faithfully before you speak faithfully.

The Two-Part Structure

Each unit follows a deliberate pattern designed to form you before you instruct others:

Personal Bible Study (Before Sermon Preparation)

This private first step slows you down. Read the passage repeatedly. Notice what it actually says. Let it speak to you before you speak for it.

Primary Scripture (ESV) identifies the governing passage.

Read the Passage Slowly resists hurried preparation.

Observe What the Text Says models careful exegesis.

Identify the Central Truth finds the passage's main burden.

Let Scripture Interpret Scripture shows the Bible's harmony.

Personal Reflection and Prayer invites transformation first in you.

Some studies may never become sermons and this is by design. The Word has still done its work.

Sermon Training Outline
(For Public Teaching)

Only after personal study comes this framework. It is not a manuscript.

Primary Biblical Text and Big Idea restate your discovery

Exegetical Observations show how text supports meaning

Christ-Centered Focus guards against moralism

Adventist Theological Trajectory connects to our message

Sermon Movement provides simple structure

Pastoral Application and Training Notes guide without scripting

Expand it through prayer and your own engagement with the congregation.

A Word of Encouragement

You may feel under-prepared. Resources may be limited. Yet your calling is real. Scripture remains accessible, and the Holy Spirit remains present. This book assumes your faithfulness is sufficient. Study slowly. Pray honestly. Let the text shape you. The church needs servants formed by the Word, not performers seeking approval.

Not every study will become a sermon. Some passages may do their work privately and never reach the pulpit. That outcome is not failure. It is faithfulness.

Quick Start for Elders

(30 Minutes This Week)

If time is short, do this first.

Read

Preface (3 minutes)

Chapter 1 (5 minutes)

Pick One

Sermon Foundation #1: John 1:1–14

Do ONLY This Section

Personal Bible Study (15 minutes)

How to Study

Read the passage three times slowly

Observe: What does the text say?

Identify the central truth: What stands out?

Pray: Let the Word speak to you before you speak for it

Next Week (If Ready)

Move to the Sermon Training Outline

Some studies never become sermons. That is faithfulness.

Why the English Standard Version (ESV)

All Scripture in this book is taken from the English Standard Version (ESV). The ESV is a word for word translation that preserves the structure and movement of the biblical text. This makes it especially suitable for training purposes, where clarity, accuracy, and faithfulness to the original text are essential.

A Word to the Reader

You do not need to be a pastor to teach the Bible, and you do not need advanced degrees to be faithful. What you do need is humility, discipline, and a willingness to learn. The church has never depended solely on professional speakers for its spiritual life. It has always been sustained by servants who allowed the Word of God to shape them first.

The church does not need more performers. It needs servants formed by the Word of God.

PART I:

FORMATION BEFORE FUNCTION

Chapter 1
Called to Serve: Adventist Identity and the Role of the Local Elder

The role of the local elder within the Seventh-day Adventist Church is rooted in calling, not convenience. Elders are not substitutes for pastors when clergy are absent, nor are they temporary solutions to logistical challenges. They are spiritual leaders recognized by the church and entrusted with responsibility for teaching, visitation, encouragement, and spiritual oversight.[2]

The Seventh-day Adventist Church has formally articulated this responsibility through its Church Manual and Elder's Manual, which outline the authority, duties, and expectations entrusted to local elders. These documents provide essential guidance for order, accountability, and faithful leadership within the local church.[3]

---

[2] Seventh-day Adventist Church, *Church Manual*, 21st ed., rev. 2025 (Silver Spring, MD: General Conference of Seventh-day Adventists, 2025), 77–84.

[3] Seventh-day Adventist Church, *Church Manual*, 21st ed., rev. 2025 (Silver Spring, MD: General Conference of Seventh-day Adventists, 2025), 71–76; see also Ministerial Association, General Conference of Seventh-day Adventists, *Elder's Manual* (Silver Spring, MD: General Conference of Seventh-day Adventists, 2010), 9–15.

In many congregations, elders do not serve alone. Lay leaders often assist in preaching, teaching, visitation, and spiritual nurture, particularly in contexts where pastoral presence is limited or responsibilities are widely shared. While the local elder remains the recognized spiritual leader of the congregation, these lay servants participate in ministry under the guidance and accountability of the church. Their service reflects the Adventist conviction that every believer is called to share in the mission of the church according to their gifts, preparation, and circumstances.

Adventist identity shapes this calling. From its earliest days, the movement emphasized the priesthood of all believers and the shared responsibility of the church. Elders were expected to know Scripture, to live consistently with it, and to help others understand it. Preaching, teaching, visitation, and outreach were not separate tasks. They were expressions of the same spiritual responsibility.

This book does not replace the guidance provided by official church manuals, nor does it seek to redefine the elder's role. Instead, it addresses a related and complementary concern: how those entrusted with these responsibilities are formed by Scripture before they carry them out.[4]

When elders speak from Scripture, they do so not as performers, but as stewards. Their authority does not come from personality or eloquence, but from faithfulness to the Word of God and accountability to the body of believers they serve. This understanding protects both the speaker and the congregation. It places Scripture at the center and keeps ministry rooted in humility.

A Word on Authority, Limits, and Pastoral Partnership

Elders are spiritual leaders, but they are not independent authorities. Christ is the Head of the church, and Scripture is the final authority, yet God also protects His people through order, accountability, and shared oversight. In practical terms, this means elders do not carry every burden alone, and they should not feel pressure to speak confidently on matters they have not studied carefully.

In healthy churches, elders and pastors work together. Elders provide continuity through presence, discipleship, and steady teaching. Pastors provide broader over-

---

[4] Ministerial Association, General Conference of Seventh-day Adventists, *Elder's Manual* (Silver Spring, MD: General Conference of Seventh-day Adventists, 2010), 3–8, 19–23.

sight, training, and support, especially when complex pastoral care, public conflict, discipline processes, or doctrinal confusion emerges. When an elder reaches the edge of what he knows, the faithful response is not to pretend. The faithful response is to slow down, return to Scripture, and ask for help.

If you are called to teach, you are also called to learn. And if you are called to lead, you are also called to remain accountable. When the church sees humble restraint, it learns that faithfulness is more important than performance.

Prayer Before Moving Forward

Lord, keep me humble. Guard me from speaking beyond Scripture and beyond my understanding. Give me courage to learn, patience to study, and wisdom to seek counsel when needed (James 3:1, ESV).

Chapter 2
A Movement Born of Scripture

The Seventh day Adventist movement did not arise from institutional planning, ecclesiastical hierarchy, or cultural momentum. It emerged from sustained and often difficult engagement with Scripture. Early Adventists were not united by formal creeds or centralized leadership, but by a shared conviction that the Bible could be understood through careful study, prayer, and comparison of Scripture with Scripture. William Miller described this conviction in personal terms, explaining that he resolved "to lay aside all commentaries, and use only the Scriptures," allowing the Bible itself to guide his understanding through patient and systematic study.[5] This conviction shaped both belief and practice from the beginning.

Following the Great Disappointment of 1844, believers did not abandon Scripture in discouragement. Instead, many returned to the biblical text with renewed seriousness, seeking to understand where their interpretation had gone wrong. This process was not quick or

---

[5] William Miller, *Evidence from Scripture and History of the Second Coming of Christ* (Boston: Joshua V. Himes, 1842), 5–7.

tidy. It involved disagreement, correction, and gradual clarification. Doctrines central to Adventist identity developed over time through collective Bible study rather than authoritative decree.[6] Scripture functioned as the final authority, even when conclusions challenged existing assumptions. Joseph Bates later reflected that clarity emerged only through repeated examination of Scripture, as believers studied together, tested conclusions openly, and allowed understanding to mature rather than forcing immediate agreement.[7]

Early Adventist preaching was inseparable from Bible study. Sermons were not crafted primarily to persuade emotionally or impress rhetorically. They were extensions of communal investigation. Passages were read publicly, examined carefully, and explained patiently. Believers expected teaching to arise from the text itself rather than from personal insight or borrowed tradition. This approach required humility. Speakers often acknowledged uncertainty and allowed understanding to mature through continued study. James White described early Adventist teachers as "students of the Word," noting that they spoke cautiously, recognizing that truth

6 George R Knight, *A Brief History of Seventh day Adventists* (Hagerstown, MD: Review and Herald Publishing Association, 2012), 29.

[7] Joseph Bates, *The Seventh Day Sabbath, a Perpetual Sign* (New Bedford, MA: Benjamin Lindsey, 1846), 7–9.

unfolded progressively through continued engagement with Scripture rather than instant certainty.[8]

In the early decades of the movement, this commitment to Scripture took practical and visible form. Believers gathered to read passages aloud, questioned interpretations openly, and allowed understanding to mature through discussion rather than decree. Camp meetings often functioned as extended Bible study schools where teaching unfolded over days and weeks. Literature evangelists spent evenings discussing doctrines encountered in homes, refining their understanding through dialogue. This was not professionalism. It was discipleship. And it proved effective. Doctrines now central to Adventist identity, including the Sabbath, the sanctuary, and the investigative judgment, emerged through careful, communal wrestling with Scripture rather than top down pronouncement.[9] J. N. Andrews exemplified this method by insisting that doctrine must rest on "the plain testimony of Scripture," tested through sustained comparison of biblical passages rather than accepted on reputation or tradition.[10]

----

[8] James White, "Unity of the Church," *Review and Herald*, June 1, 1850, 84–85.

[9] George R Knight, *A Brief History of Seventh day Adventists* (Hagerstown, MD: Review and Herald Publishing Association, 2012), 29.

[10] J. N. Andrews, *The History of the Sabbath and the First Day of the*

Ellen G White repeatedly affirmed this method of formation. She warned against dependence on human opinion and urged believers to ground faith and teaching firmly in Scripture. She emphasized that ministers and lay leaders alike were to be students of the Word, allowing the Bible to shape character before shaping instruction.[11] The authority of preaching, in this view, rested not in position or eloquence, but in faithfulness to the biblical text. She cautioned that opinions, habits, and customs were not to be treated as authority, and urged believers to test every teaching by Scripture itself rather than by human judgment.[12]

This history matters for contemporary elders and lay leaders. In many settings today, especially in rural or under resourced contexts, leaders face similar conditions to those of the early movement. Access to formal theological education may be limited. Pastoral presence may be intermittent. Resources may be scarce. Yet the responsibility to teach faithfully remains. The Adventist movement was born in such conditions and flourished precisely because Scripture remained central.

Week (Battle Creek, MI: Review and Herald, 1873), vi–vii.

[11] Ellen G White, *Gospel Workers* (Washington, DC: Review and Herald Publishing Association, 1915), 100.

[12] Ellen G. White, *The Great Controversy* (Mountain View, CA: Pacific Press, 1911), 595.

Adventist identity has always assumed that ordinary believers are capable of careful Bible study. Scripture was never treated as the possession of specialists alone. While education and training were valued, they were understood as supports rather than substitutes for personal engagement with the Word. This conviction safeguards the church from dependence on personalities and protects doctrine from drifting with cultural trends.

At the same time, early Adventists understood that Scripture must be handled responsibly. Private interpretation was never meant to operate in isolation from the community of faith. Beliefs were tested publicly, refined collectively, and corrected when necessary. Scripture interpreted Scripture within the gathered body of believers. This balance between personal study and communal accountability remains essential for faithful leadership today.

For elders and lay leaders, this history offers both encouragement and caution. It affirms that faithful teaching does not require professional polish or advanced credentials. It does require discipline, patience, and humility before the Word. It cautions against rushed preparation, overconfidence, and reliance on secondhand material. The movement was not sustained by shortcuts. It was sustained by perseverance in study.

To be an Adventist leader is to stand within this heritage. Preaching and teaching are not performances to be perfected, but trusts to be stewarded. Scripture remains the foundation, not merely the source material. When leaders approach the Bible with reverence and care, they participate in the same formative process that gave birth to the movement itself.

Lord, You have called this church into existence through Your Word. Teach us to study with humility, to listen before we speak, and to trust Your Spirit to lead us into truth. Make this church a true training school for Christian workers, formed not by pride or haste, but by faithfulness to Scripture (Psalm 119:18, ESV).

Interlude:
From William Miller to Today

Early Adventists modeled the same pattern this book follows. Deep personal study came before public ministry. God formed servants through Scripture before entrusting them with leadership. This pattern was not accidental, but cultivated through deliberate habits of study and prayer.

William Miller devoted himself to careful Bible study long before he ever preached publicly. With limited formal education, he spent approximately fourteen years comparing Scripture with Scripture, allowing the Bible to interpret itself. His preaching flowed from conviction shaped by patient study rather than institutional credentials.[13] His experience illustrates how disciplined personal study can prepare ordinary believers for faithful public ministry.

Ellen G. White consistently redirected believers back to Scripture as the foundation of faith and service. She wrote, "Every church should be a training school for

---

[13] F. D. Nichol, *The Midnight Cry: A Defense of the Character and Conduct of William Miller* (Washington, DC: Review and Herald, 1944), 20–22.

Christian workers."[14] Her role did not replace Bible study but guarded and strengthened a people already formed by the Word.[15] Training, in this sense, meant forming character and habits of study before developing public ability.

J. N. Andrews represents the maturing of disciplined lay study into rigorous scholarship and mission. Largely self-taught, Andrews read the Bible through repeatedly and combined deep biblical understanding with faithful service as the church's first official overseas missionary.[16] His life demonstrates how careful study can grow into responsible leadership and global service without abandoning humility before Scripture.

These pioneers demonstrate a consistent truth. Formation precedes function. Scripture shaped them before mission sent them. They were students of the Word before they became teachers of the church. That same pathway remains open to elders and lay leaders today.

---

[14] Ellen G. White, *The Ministry of Healing* (Mountain View, CA: Pacific Press, 1905), 149.

[15] Gilbert M. Valentine, *The Shaping of Adventism: The Case of W. C. White and the Ellen G. White Estate* (Berrien Springs, MI: Andrews University Press, 1992), 45–47.

[16] Gilbert Valentine, "John N. Andrews Symposium," *Adventist Heritage* 9, no. 1 (1984): 12.

Chapter 3
Why Training Matters More Than Sermons

In many congregations, elders and lay leaders are asked to preach simply because someone must speak. A Sabbath arrives, a service must be led, and words are required. Over time, this pattern can quietly reshape how Scripture is approached. The Bible becomes material to be assembled rather than truth to be received. Preaching shifts from stewardship to task fulfillment.

When this happens, even sincere leaders may begin to rely on familiar outlines, recycled messages, or borrowed sermons. Preparation becomes compressed. Study becomes selective. Prayer becomes functional rather than formative. The problem is not a lack of devotion, but a lack of training. Without formation, responsibility slowly turns into pressure, and pressure often produces shortcuts.

Training addresses this problem at its root. Training does not promise eloquence or guarantee immediate results. It cultivates habits of careful study, disciplined reflection, and patient listening to Scripture. These habits sustain leaders over years rather than weeks. Sermons are momentary. Formation endures.

Ellen G White consistently warned against superficial preparation for sacred responsibilities. She emphasized that those who teach the Word must themselves be shaped by it, allowing Scripture to refine character and judgment before it is shared publicly.[17] Training, in this sense, is not professionalization. It is faithfulness. It prepares leaders to handle Scripture with care rather than confidence alone.

The distinction between training and sermon preparation is subtle but significant. Sermon preparation focuses on producing something to say. Training focuses on shaping the one who speaks. When training is neglected, preaching becomes performance driven, even when intentions are sincere. When training is prioritized, preaching becomes an overflow of disciplined study and lived conviction.

This distinction matters especially in contexts where pastors rotate frequently or serve multiple congregations. In such settings, the stability of the local church often depends on elders who are prepared to teach consistently

---

[17] Ellen G White, *Testimonies for the Church*, vol. 5 (Mountain View, CA: Pacific Press Publishing Association, 1889), 254.

and responsibly. A well trained elder provides continuity grounded in Scripture rather than personality. The church is strengthened not by novelty, but by faithfulness.

Scripture itself affirms the importance of preparation that goes beyond public speaking. Paul reminded Timothy that Scripture equips the servant of God for every good work, not merely for effective communication (2 Timothy 3:16–17, ESV). The goal of training is not to produce speakers, but servants who are thoroughly equipped for ministry in its many forms.

Training also protects leaders from overreach. Without it, individuals may speak beyond their understanding or address issues without sufficient biblical grounding. With training, leaders learn to recognize the limits of their knowledge and to speak with appropriate restraint. Silence, when guided by humility, can be as faithful as speech.

For elders and lay leaders, embracing training is an act of trust. It trusts that God works through slow, faithful processes rather than hurried results. It trusts that Scripture accomplishes its purpose even when no sermon is produced. It trusts that formation matters more than visibility.

This book prioritizes training because the health of the church depends on leaders who are formed by the Word before they speak from it. Sermons will come. Opportunities will arise. What endures is the character and faithfulness of those entrusted with the Word of God.

Lord, guard us from haste and from the pressure to speak before we have listened. Form us by Your Word before we teach it to others. Give us patience to study faithfully, courage to wait when understanding is incomplete, and humility to serve Your church with care rather than confidence alone (2 Timothy 2:15, ESV).

Interlude:
When You Do Not Know Yet

There is a quiet pressure in ministry that most people never see. It is the pressure to have an answer for every question, a verse for every situation, and clarity for every decision. But Scripture does not call leaders to know everything. Scripture calls leaders to be faithful, to be teachable, and to be honest.

Some of the most dangerous moments in teaching are not when a person lacks sincerity, but when a person feels rushed to speak. When that rush takes over, leaders can start borrowing certainty. They repeat what sounds strong, even if they have not tested it. Over time, this does not build confidence. It builds fragility.

A faithful elder can say, I do not know yet. I need to study more. That is not weakness. That is reverence. It is also protection for the church. God is not threatened by slow understanding. He is honored by patient study.

Prayer Before Moving Forward

Lord, teach me to love truth more than approval. Give me the humility to pause, the discipline to study, and the courage to admit what I do not yet understand (Psalm 119:18, ESV).

PART II

HOW ADVENTISTS READ SCRIPTURE

Why Method Matters

A method is not a replacement for the Holy Spirit. It is a guardrail. It helps a sincere believer avoid careless conclusions, emotional proof texting, and confident error. A method slows the reader down so the text can speak before the teacher speaks.

This matters because elders are often asked to teach in real life conditions. Limited time, limited resources, spiritual need, and real people carrying real burdens. In those conditions, the temptation is not usually open rebellion. The temptation is haste. A faithful method protects the church from haste, and it protects the elder from pressure.

The chapters that follow describe the posture and practices that have historically kept Adventist Bible study grounded. They are not academic obstacles. They are pastoral safeguards.

Chapter 4
Approaching the Bible with Reverence and Humility

Faithful study of Scripture begins not with technique, but with posture. The Bible is not approached as an object to be mastered, but as the living Word through which God speaks. Reverence does not mean fear or passivity. It means attentiveness, care, and willingness to listen before drawing conclusions. Humility recognizes that understanding develops over time and that correction is part of spiritual growth.

Throughout Adventist history, Bible study has been understood as a spiritual discipline before it is a teaching task. Early believers approached Scripture prayerfully, trusting that the same Spirit who inspired the Word would guide sincere study. This dependence shaped both interpretation and character. Without prayer, study risks becoming technical and detached from transformation.

Ellen G White repeatedly emphasized that Scripture should never be handled casually. She warned that intellectual ability alone is insufficient for understanding divine truth and that pride can obscure spiritual discernment. Those who approach the Bible with self-confidence rather than submission place themselves at risk of distortion.[18] Reverent study begins with a recognition of personal limitation and dependence on God.

Humility in study also involves patience. Scripture does not always yield immediate clarity. Some passages invite prolonged reflection, comparison, and prayer. Adventist interpretation has historically allowed time for understanding to mature rather than forcing premature conclusions. This restraint protects against speculative teaching and overconfidence.

Scripture itself affirms the necessity of a humble posture. The psalmist prayed for understanding before instruction, acknowledging dependence on God for insight (Psalm 119:18, ESV). Jesus likewise affirmed that spiritual truth is revealed to those who approach with childlike trust rather than self-assurance (Matthew 11:25, ESV). These passages remind the reader that comprehension is a gift, not an achievement.

For elders and lay leaders, reverence and humility are safeguards. They protect the church from careless teaching and protect the teacher from speaking beyond understanding. Leaders who are willing to say I do not yet

---

[18] Ellen G White, *Education* (Mountain View, CA: Pacific Press Publishing Association, 1903), 189.

understand model faithfulness rather than weakness. Such honesty builds trust and encourages continued study within the congregation.

Approaching Scripture with reverence and humility also shapes how it is taught. The goal is not to impress listeners with insight, but to invite them into the same posture of attentiveness and trust. Teaching becomes an act of shared submission to the Word rather than an exercise in authority.

This posture prepares the reader for faithful study. Before tools are used and methods applied, the heart must be oriented rightly. Reverence opens the ear. Humility keeps the teacher teachable. Together, they form the foundation for all responsible handling of Scripture.

Chapter 5
Exegesis and the Danger of Reading Ourselves into the Text

Faithful Bible study seeks to draw meaning from the text rather than impose meaning upon it. This process, commonly referred to as exegesis, requires discipline, restraint, and careful attention to context. Its opposite, eisegesis, occurs when readers import assumptions, experiences, or preferences into the text and then attribute those ideas to Scripture itself.

The danger of eisegesis is often subtle. Readers may approach Scripture with sincere intentions and strong convictions, yet unknowingly allow personal perspectives to govern interpretation. When this happens, the Bible begins to mirror the reader rather than challenge them. Over time, Scripture loses its corrective function and becomes a tool for self-affirmation.

Adventist interpretation has historically emphasized the importance of allowing Scripture to speak on its own terms. Early believers compared passage with passage, resisted isolated proof texting, and allowed clearer texts to illuminate more difficult ones. This approach helped guard against speculative conclusions and theological imbalance.[19] Exegesis, in this tradition, was understood as an act of listening rather than control.

Ellen G White repeatedly cautioned against approaching Scripture with predetermined conclusions. She warned that readers who seek confirmation rather than understanding are especially vulnerable to error. When personal opinion becomes the lens through which Scripture is read, truth is distorted and humility is lost.[20] Faithful exegesis requires a willingness to be corrected by the Word.

Scripture itself warns against this tendency. Peter acknowledged that some biblical writings are difficult to understand and can be twisted by those who are unstable or untaught (2 Peter 3:16, ESV). This warning is not directed at malicious intent, but at careless handling. It underscores the need for patience, accountability, and restraint in interpretation.

For elders and lay leaders, the discipline of exegesis is essential. Teaching that arises from imposed meaning may sound confident, but it lacks biblical authority. Faithful

---

[19] George R Knight, *A Brief History of Seventh day Adventists* (Hagerstown, MD: Review and Herald Publishing Association, 2012), 31.

[20] Ellen G White, *The Great Controversy* (Mountain View, CA: Pacific Press Publishing Association, 1911), 599.

leaders learn to ask what the text says before asking how it applies. Observation precedes interpretation. Interpretation precedes application. Skipping these steps increases the risk of distortion.

Exegesis also requires openness to communal correction. Adventist study has never been purely individualistic. Understanding is tested within the body of believers, refined through dialogue, and corrected when necessary. This communal process helps expose blind spots and protects against private interpretations that drift from the broader witness of Scripture.

By resisting the urge to read ourselves into the text, leaders allow Scripture to retain its formative power. The Word confronts, instructs, and reshapes the reader. This posture may be uncomfortable at times, but it is essential for faithful leadership. The authority of teaching rests not in personal insight, but in submission to what God has already spoken.

Chapter 6
Context Matters

Every passage of Scripture belongs to a larger whole. Words are shaped by sentences, sentences by paragraphs, and paragraphs by books. Meaning does not arise in isolation. When texts are removed from their literary, historical, or canonical context, interpretation becomes unstable. Faithful Bible study therefore requires attention to context as a primary discipline rather than an optional supplement.

Adventist interpretation has long emphasized the importance of reading Scripture within its immediate and broader settings. Early believers recognized that isolated proof texts could be used to support nearly any position if detached from context. By examining passages in relation to their surrounding argument and to the rest of Scripture, they sought to preserve coherence and theological balance.[21] Context functioned as a safeguard against distortion.

---

[21] George R Knight, *A Brief History of Seventh day Adventists* (Hagerstown, MD: Review and Herald Publishing Association, 2012), 33.

Literary context concerns how a passage fits within the flow of thought of a particular book. Authors write with purpose, progression, and emphasis. Ignoring that movement risks misunderstanding intent. Historical context considers the circumstances in which a text was written, including audience, culture, and situation. These factors inform meaning without overriding it. Context clarifies what a passage addresses and what it does not.

Canonical context ensures that individual texts are read in harmony with the whole of Scripture. Adventists have consistently affirmed that Scripture interprets Scripture and that no passage contradicts the broader biblical witness. Difficult or obscure texts are understood in light of clearer teaching. This approach resists sensational interpretation and promotes doctrinal stability.

Ellen G White strongly affirmed the necessity of contextual reading. She warned against using isolated passages to support preconceived ideas and emphasized that truth is revealed through careful, connected study of Scripture.[22] When texts are separated from their setting, she noted, they often lose their intended meaning and are misapplied.

------

[22] Ellen G White, *Selected Messages*, book 1 (Washington, DC: Review and Herald Publishing Association, 1958), 42.

Scripture itself models contextual awareness. Jesus frequently appealed to the broader testimony of Scripture when addressing questions of doctrine and practice. He resisted interpretations that ignored context and corrected readings that failed to account for the full scope of God's revelation (Matthew 22:29, ESV). His example reinforces the responsibility of readers to handle Scripture thoughtfully.

For elders and lay leaders, attentiveness to context promotes humility and clarity. It slows the pace of study and guards against confident error. Context reminds the teacher that Scripture speaks with intention and coherence. Teaching that respects context honors both the text and the congregation.

When leaders commit to contextual study, Scripture is allowed to speak fully. Meaning becomes clearer. Application becomes more faithful. The Bible retains its authority not because it is quoted often, but because it is understood carefully.

Chapter 7
Scripture Interpreting Scripture

One of the most enduring principles of Adventist Bible study is that Scripture interprets Scripture. The Bible is understood to be internally coherent, unified by the same divine Author, and consistent in its testimony. Clear passages illuminate more difficult ones. Themes develop across books and testaments. When read together, Scripture explains itself.

This principle emerged naturally in the early Adventist movement. Believers compared texts carefully, tracing themes and allowing repeated patterns to clarify meaning. Rather than relying on external authority to resolve interpretive questions, they returned to Scripture itself. This practice fostered patience and discouraged speculative conclusions.[23]

Scripture interpreting Scripture does not mean collecting verses at random. It requires discernment and restraint. Cross references must respect context and genre. Historical narratives, poetry, prophecy, and epistles communicate truth in different ways. Responsible comparison

---

[23] George R Knight, *Reading Ellen White* (Hagerstown, MD: Review and Herald Publishing Association, 1997), 63.

honors these distinctions while recognizing the unity of the biblical message.

Ellen G White strongly supported this method of study. She urged believers to let the Bible be its own expositor and warned against interpretations that relied on isolated texts or human reasoning alone. When Scripture is allowed to explain itself, she observed, truth becomes clearer and error is exposed.[24]

The Bible itself encourages this approach. Isaiah invited readers to test teaching by comparing it with what God had already revealed (Isaiah 8:20, ESV). Jesus and the apostles frequently appealed to earlier Scripture to explain later events, demonstrating continuity rather than contradiction. This internal dialogue within Scripture reinforces confidence in its unity.

For elders and lay leaders, this principle provides both freedom and responsibility. It frees the teacher from dependence on novelty or speculation. It also requires discipline, since not every perceived connection is valid. Faithful leaders learn to trace themes patiently and to allow Scripture to set its own boundaries.

----

[24] Ellen G White, *The Great Controversy* (Mountain View, CA: Pacific Press Publishing Association, 1911), 521.

Scripture interpreting Scripture also cultivates humility. No single passage carries the full weight of doctrine. Truth emerges through the harmony of the whole. This approach resists extremes and promotes balance, particularly in areas of prophecy and doctrine that invite strong opinions.

When Scripture is allowed to interpret itself, teaching remains grounded and Christ centered. The Bible speaks with clarity and coherence. Leaders become guides rather than authorities. The church is strengthened as Scripture retains its rightful place as the final measure of truth.

PART III
TOOLS FOR FAITHFUL STUDY

Chapter 8
Observation Before Application

Faithful Bible study begins with careful observation. Before asking what a passage means or how it applies, the reader must first attend to what the text actually says. Faithful Bible study follows a deliberate order: observation listens to the text, interpretation explains the text, and application lives out the truth of the text. Observation is the discipline of noticing details without immediately assigning meaning. It slows the pace of study and guards against assumption.

By observation, one intentionally practices paying attention to the text as it stands, without explanation or evaluation. This includes reading a passage repeatedly, noting what is present rather than why it is present, and resisting the urge to interpret too quickly. Observation asks simple but essential questions such as: What is happening? Who is speaking? What words or ideas are emphasized? What connections are visible within the passage itself?

Observation includes attention to repeated words, key phrases, contrasts, progression of thought, and emphasis. These features are not accidental. Biblical authors communicate meaning through structure as well as content. When readers overlook these elements, interpretation becomes detached from the intent of the text.

At this stage, the reader does not attempt to explain the significance of these details. Observation records what is seen without drawing conclusions. Meaning will come later through interpretation. Observation simply ensures that interpretation is anchored in what the text actually contains, not in what the reader expects to find.

Adventist Bible study has historically emphasized this careful attentiveness. Early believers approached Scripture patiently, reading and rereading passages before drawing conclusions. This habit protected against speculative interpretation and fostered clarity over time.[25] Observation allowed Scripture to speak before human reasoning attempted to explain it.

Ellen G White encouraged this kind of deliberate engagement with Scripture. She urged believers to study carefully, comparing passage with passage, and to resist the temptation to move too quickly to application. She warned that careless reading often leads to misunderstanding and superficial teaching.[26] Observation, in her

---

[25] George R Knight, *A Brief History of Seventh day Adventists* (Hagerstown, MD: Review and Herald Publishing Association, 2012), 34.

[26] Ellen G White, *Counsels to Parents, Teachers, and Students* (Mountain

counsel, was a spiritual discipline that required effort and restraint.

Her counsel consistently emphasized that hasty conclusions often arise not from lack of intelligence, but from lack of attentiveness. Careful observation, she taught, creates space for the Holy Spirit to guide understanding rather than allowing impulse or familiarity to govern interpretation.[27]

Scripture itself models the importance of observation. Ezra is described as one who set his heart to study the Law of the Lord before teaching it to others (Ezra 7:10, ESV). His example reflects an intentional sequence. Study precedes explanation. Understanding precedes instruction.

Ezra's pattern reflects the purpose of observation. He gave himself first to attentive study before seeking to explain or apply the law. This sequence reminds leaders that authority in teaching grows out of careful listening to the text, not quick conclusions drawn from it.

For elders and lay leaders, observation is especially important. Teaching that bypasses careful observation may sound practical but lacks depth. When leaders train

---

View, CA: Pacific Press Publishing Association, 1913), 461.

[27] Ellen G. White, *Education* (Mountain View, CA: Pacific Press, 1903), 189–190.

themselves to notice what Scripture emphasizes, their teaching becomes more faithful and less driven by preference or habit.

Observation does not eliminate the need for interpretation or application. It prepares for them. By anchoring study in what the text actually says, leaders allow Scripture to govern meaning rather than personal experience or expectation. This discipline forms habits of patience and attentiveness that strengthen long term faithfulness.

When observation is prioritized, Scripture retains its authority. The reader listens before speaking. The teacher learns before instructing. This posture protects both the integrity of the text and the spiritual health of the church.

Chapter 9
Word Studies Without Abuse

Word studies can be valuable tools when used carefully and humbly. They help clarify meaning, confirm understanding, and illuminate patterns within Scripture. However, when misused, they can distort meaning rather than reveal it. Faithful study requires restraint as well as curiosity.

A biblical word study is the careful examination of how a word is used within a specific passage of Scripture in order to better understand the author's intended meaning. Rather than beginning with a dictionary definition, faithful word studies begin with the text itself, allowing context, flow of thought, and purpose to shape how a word is understood. The aim is not to uncover hidden meanings, but to gain clarity about what the inspired writer is communicating.

A common danger in word studies is the assumption that a word carries the same meaning in every context. Biblical words, like words in any language, derive meaning from how they are used within a sentence and passage. Isolating a word from its context and assigning it a preferred definition risks misinterpretation.

For this reason, responsible word studies follow a clear order. The passage is first read carefully to grasp its overall message. Only then is a specific word examined to see how it functions within that message. Language tools such as concordances or lexicons are consulted afterward, not to determine meaning independently, but to confirm or refine what careful observation has already revealed.

Adventist interpreters have historically exercised caution in the use of language tools. Early believers relied primarily on context and comparison of Scripture with Scripture, using word studies as confirmation rather than foundation. This restraint helped maintain balance and prevented technical tools from overshadowing the text itself.[28]

Ellen G White warned against overreliance on linguistic detail detached from context. She cautioned that an emphasis on technical knowledge without spiritual discernment can lead to pride and confusion. True understanding, she affirmed, arises when tools serve the Word rather than dominate it.[29]

---

[28] George R Knight, *Reading Ellen White* (Hagerstown, MD: Review and Herald Publishing Association, 1997), 67.

[29] Ellen G White, *Selected Messages*, book 1 (Washington, DC: Review and Herald Publishing Association, 1958), 19.

Her concern was not with careful study itself, but with allowing technique to replace humility, prayer, and submission to Scripture. She repeatedly emphasized that intellectual ability alone is insufficient for rightly understanding God's Word apart from the guidance of the Holy Spirit.[30]

Scripture encourages careful handling of truth. Paul instructed Timothy to rightly handle the word of truth, implying both diligence and responsibility (2 Timothy 2:15, ESV). This responsibility includes knowing when deeper analysis is helpful and when it is unnecessary.

Not every passage requires a word study. In many cases, the meaning of a text is plain through careful reading and attention to context. Word studies are most beneficial when a term is repeated, carries theological weight, or plays a central role in the author's argument. Wise leaders learn to discern when deeper analysis serves the text and when it distracts from it.

For elders and lay leaders, word studies should remain servants, not masters. Not every word requires analysis. In many cases, the meaning of a passage is clear through

[30] Ellen G. White, *Selected Messages*, book 1 (Washington, DC: Review and Herald, 1958), 411–412

context alone. Language tools are most useful when they confirm what careful observation has already revealed.

Used properly, word studies deepen appreciation for Scripture and reinforce confidence in its coherence. Used improperly, they create false precision and distract from the central message of the text. Faithful leaders learn to use these tools sparingly, always submitting conclusions to the larger context of Scripture.

By practicing restraint, leaders protect themselves and their congregations from confusion. The goal is not to display technical skill, but to understand and communicate God's Word faithfully. When word studies remain anchored in humility and context, they serve the purpose for which they were intended.

Chapter 10
Studying Scripture with the Whole Person

Faithful Bible study engages more than the intellect alone. Scripture addresses the whole person, including mind, heart, memory, and lived experience. God speaks through words that are understood cognitively, yet those words also shape character, affections, and daily life.

Adventist theology has long affirmed that understanding develops over time through repeated engagement with Scripture. Early believers revisited passages, reflected on experience, and allowed insights to mature. This process acknowledged that growth in understanding often occurs gradually rather than instantaneously.[31]

Ellen G White emphasized that Scripture should be studied thoughtfully and reflectively. She encouraged believers to meditate on God's Word, allowing it to shape motives and conduct. She warned that hurried study may inform the mind without transforming the

---

[31] George R Knight, *A Brief History of Seventh day Adventists* (Hagerstown, MD: Review and Herald Publishing Association, 2012), 35.

life.[32] Studying with the whole person invites Scripture to work deeply rather than superficially.

Scripture itself affirms this holistic engagement. The psalmist described God's Word as a lamp that guides daily living, not merely abstract thought (Psalm 119:105, ESV). James likewise urged believers to receive the Word with humility and to allow it to produce obedient action (James 1:21–22, ESV). These texts emphasize integration between understanding and practice.

For elders and lay leaders, studying Scripture with the whole person fosters authenticity. Teaching that arises from lived engagement carries weight and credibility. When leaders allow Scripture to shape their own lives, their instruction becomes grounded and sincere.

This approach also encourages patience. Not every passage yields immediate clarity. Reflection, prayer, and experience often contribute to understanding over time. Writing notes, revisiting texts, and reflecting on application help integrate Scripture into daily life.

Studying Scripture with the whole person guards against both intellectualism and emotionalism. It affirms thoughtful study while recognizing the role of experi-

---

[32] Ellen G White, *Steps to Christ* (Mountain View, CA: Pacific Press Publishing Association, 1892), 90.

ence and reflection. When Scripture is allowed to address the whole person, it forms leaders who teach with integrity and live with consistency.

Ultimately, this holistic engagement honors the purpose of Scripture itself. God's Word is given not merely to inform, but to transform. Leaders who study in this way are shaped by the Word before they speak from it, strengthening both their ministry and the church they serve.

Chapter 11
Notes, Outlines, and Long Term Habits

Faithful Bible study is sustained not by intention alone, but by habit. Notes, outlines, and consistent study practices help preserve insight and protect understanding over time. Without structure, even meaningful study can fade quickly, leaving little to build upon in future preparation.

Adventist leaders have historically valued disciplined habits of study. Early believers recorded insights, traced themes across Scripture, and revisited passages repeatedly. These practices supported careful thinking and encouraged continuity of understanding rather than dependence on memory alone.[33] Notes functioned as tools of stewardship, helping believers retain and refine what Scripture revealed.

Ellen G White affirmed the value of written reflection in spiritual growth. She encouraged believers to write down thoughts from Scripture, recognizing that reflection deepens understanding and strengthens memory.

[33] George R Knight, *A Brief History of Seventh day Adventists* (Hagerstown, MD: Review and Herald Publishing Association, 2012), 36.

She warned that neglecting such habits often results in shallow engagement with the Word.[34] Writing slows the mind and clarifies thought.

Outlines serve a similar purpose. They help organize observations, clarify relationships within a passage, and reveal the movement of thought. An outline does not replace study. It records it. When used faithfully, outlines help leaders distinguish between what the text emphasizes and what the reader assumes.

Long term habits protect leaders during seasons of pressure or fatigue. When study becomes irregular, teaching often becomes reactive rather than reflective. Established habits provide stability when time is limited and responsibilities are heavy. They allow Scripture to remain central even when preparation time is constrained.

Scripture affirms the value of disciplined reflection. The psalmist speaks of meditating on God's law day and night, allowing it to shape life and conduct (Psalm 1:2, ESV). Such meditation assumes regular engagement rather than occasional exposure. Habits form faithfulness.

---

[34] Ellen G White, *Counsels on Sabbath School Work* (Washington, DC: Review and Herald Publishing Association, 1913), 34.

For elders and lay leaders, notes and outlines are not academic luxuries. They are practical supports for long term ministry. They preserve insight, encourage accountability, and provide a record of growth. Over time, they form a personal library of reflection shaped by Scripture rather than convenience.

Sustainable ministry depends on sustainable practices. Notes, outlines, and habits serve the leader quietly and consistently. They support faithful study long before teaching occurs. In this way, preparation becomes a rhythm rather than a crisis, strengthening both the leader and the church.

PART IV
FROM STUDY TO PROCLAMATION

Chapter 12
When Study Becomes Teaching

Teaching Scripture is a sacred trust. When study moves from private engagement to public instruction, responsibility deepens. What is shared publicly carries influence and shapes understanding. For this reason, faithful leaders recognize that not every insight is meant for immediate proclamation.

Adventist practice has long emphasized that teaching flows from tested understanding. Early believers studied Scripture collectively, allowed insights to be examined, and spoke publicly only what had been weighed carefully. This process guarded the church against premature conclusions and doctrinal instability.[35] Study preceded speech.

Ellen G White repeatedly warned against speaking hastily on sacred subjects. She counseled leaders to ensure that their understanding was clear and grounded before presenting truth to others. Words spoken without sufficient preparation, she noted, can confuse rather than

---

[35] George R Knight, *A Brief History of Seventh day Adventists* (Hagerstown, MD: Review and Herald Publishing Association, 2012), 38.

enlighten.[36] Teaching requires discernment as well as knowledge.

Scripture itself reinforces this caution. James warned that those who teach will be judged with greater strictness, highlighting the weight of influence carried by instruction (James 3:1, ESV). This warning is not meant to discourage teaching, but to encourage humility and careful preparation.

When study becomes teaching, the goal shifts from personal formation to communal edification. Leaders must consider clarity, accuracy, and spiritual impact. Teaching should reflect what Scripture says, not merely what the teacher finds interesting or persuasive.

For elders and lay leaders, this transition requires prayerful restraint. Faithful leaders learn to speak only where understanding is solid and to remain silent where questions remain. Silence, guided by humility, honors Scripture as much as speech guided by clarity.

Teaching that arises from careful study builds trust within the congregation. It communicates respect for the Word and for those who hear it. When leaders allow Scripture to shape them privately before sharing it pub-

---

[36] Ellen G White, *Evangelism* (Washington, DC: Review and Herald Publishing Association, 1946), 204.

licly, teaching becomes an act of stewardship rather than display.

Study becomes teaching when conviction is clear, understanding is tested, and the Spirit leads. This process protects the church and honors the responsibility entrusted to those who open the Word before others.

Chapter 13
Christ Centered and Adventist Faithful

All Scripture points to Christ. From creation to restoration, the Bible bears witness to God's saving work through His Son. Faithful Adventist teaching holds Christ at the center while remaining rooted in the distinctive truths entrusted to the movement.

Early Adventists understood doctrine as a means of clarifying the gospel, not replacing it. Teachings such as the Sabbath, the sanctuary, judgment, and the Second Coming were never intended to stand apart from Christ's redemptive work. Rather, they were understood to reveal His character, mission, and ongoing ministry.[37] Doctrine served the gospel, and the gospel gave doctrine meaning.

Ellen G White consistently emphasized that Christ must be central in all teaching. She warned that presenting doctrine without Christ leads to dryness and imbalance. Truth, she affirmed, must be taught in its living connection to Jesus, who embodies God's revelation and pur-

---

[37] George R Knight, *The Apocalyptic Vision and the Neutering of Adventism* (Hagerstown, MD: Review and Herald Publishing Association, 2008), 58.

pose.[38] Christ centered teaching preserves both warmth and faithfulness.

Scripture itself affirms this focus. Jesus declared that the Scriptures testify about Him, even when addressing writings that predate His incarnation (John 5:39, ESV). Paul likewise determined to know nothing among believers except Jesus Christ and Him crucified, emphasizing the centrality of the gospel (1 Corinthians 2:2, ESV).

For elders and lay leaders, Christ centered teaching requires intentionality. It resists the temptation to isolate doctrine from redemption or to present truth as abstract principle. Faithful leaders trace how biblical teaching reveals Christ's saving work and calls for response grounded in grace.

At the same time, Adventist faithfulness requires clarity. Christ centered teaching does not minimize doctrine or blur conviction. It presents truth with humility, grounded in Scripture, and oriented toward hope, redemption, and transformation.

When Christ remains central, Adventist teaching retains balance. The gospel remains primary. Doctrine finds its place. The church is nourished rather than divided.

---

[38] Ellen G White, *Gospel Workers* (Washington, DC: Review and Herald Publishing Association, 1915), 158.

Leaders serve faithfully by pointing consistently to Jesus as Savior, High Priest, and coming King.

Christ centered and Adventist faithful teaching strengthens the church's witness and deepens its hope. It reflects the unity of Scripture and honors the purpose for which truth has been entrusted to God's people.

Chapter 14
The Role of Prayer in Preaching

Prayer shapes preparation, proclamation, and response. It guards against self-reliance and keeps preaching dependent on God rather than technique. Prayer does not guarantee outcomes, but it aligns the servant with the will of God. Without prayer, preaching becomes an exercise in human effort rather than an act of spiritual stewardship.

Before Scripture is studied publicly, it must be approached privately in prayer. Prayer prepares the heart to listen before it prepares the mouth to speak. It invites the Spirit to guide understanding, correct assumptions, and deepen humility. Adventist leaders have long understood that faithful preaching begins not at the desk or pulpit, but on the knees.[39]

Prayer also shapes how Scripture is understood. It does not replace careful study or disciplined observation, but it frames them rightly. Through prayer, the reader acknowledges dependence on divine guidance and resists the temptation to control the text. This posture allows

---

[39] Ellen G White, *Gospel Workers* (Washington, DC: Review and Herald Publishing Association, 1915), 111.

Scripture to speak with authority rather than being bent to preference or agenda.

Ellen G White consistently emphasized the necessity of prayer in connection with the study and presentation of God's Word. She warned that even correct doctrine, when presented without prayerful dependence, loses spiritual power.[40] Prayer, she taught, keeps the messenger connected to the Source of truth and guards against self-confidence.

Scripture affirms this connection between prayer and faithful proclamation. Jesus Himself prayed before teaching and preaching, modeling dependence rather than self-reliance (Mark 1:35, ESV). The apostles likewise devoted themselves to prayer and the ministry of the Word, recognizing that the two could not be separated without loss (Acts 6:4, ESV).

Prayer also shapes the act of preaching itself. It influences tone, restraint, and clarity. A prayerful preacher listens for guidance even while speaking, remaining attentive to both Scripture and congregation. Prayer tempers confidence with humility and conviction with compassion.

------

[40] Ellen G White, *Testimonies for the Church*, vol. 5 (Mountain View, CA: Pacific Press Publishing Association, 1889), 161.

After preaching, prayer continues its work. The response to God's Word belongs ultimately to Him. Prayer releases the preacher from the burden of results and entrusts the hearer to the Spirit's care. Faithful preaching does not measure success by visible outcomes, but by obedience to the task entrusted.

For elders and lay leaders, prayer is not an optional discipline added to preparation. It is the environment in which preparation occurs. When prayer is neglected, preaching becomes mechanical. When prayer is central, preaching becomes an act of worship.

The role of prayer in preaching reminds the leader that the work is God's before it is theirs. Scripture is opened. Truth is spoken. Results are surrendered. In this way, prayer preserves humility, sustains faithfulness, and keeps preaching aligned with the purposes of God.

Before any sermon is preached and before any outline is opened, the call of Scripture is first a call to Christ Himself. Elders and lay leaders are invited to return often to the simplicity of the gospel, allowing love for Christ to shape both conviction and tone. Doctrine matters because it reveals Him. Preaching endures when it flows not only from correct understanding, but from devotion to the living Savior (John 15:5, ESV).

Transition to Part V
Sermon Foundations as an Extension of Personal Study

Before Scripture is preached, it must first be received. In the life of the church, sermon preparation can quietly become task driven. A date approaches. A responsibility must be fulfilled. Words are needed for a Sabbath service, a gathering, or a moment of public teaching. When this pattern repeats, even faithful leaders may begin to approach Scripture primarily as material to be shaped rather than truth to be submitted to.

This book intentionally resists that posture.

Bible study is not a preliminary step toward preaching. It is a spiritual discipline in its own right. Scripture is given first to form the servant, not to supply content for an audience. When study is reduced to sermon preparation alone, the Word is subtly shifted from authority to resource. Over time, this shift weakens both understanding and humility.

For this reason, the sermon foundations that follow are intentionally incomplete. They are not sermons. They are not shortcuts. They are not substitutes for prayerful, personal engagement with the text. They are designed to come after personal study has already begun and, at times, after it has already accomplished its purpose without ever being preached.

Each foundation assumes that the reader has first read the passage slowly, prayed honestly, and listened carefully. The goal is not to produce something to say, but to be shaped by what God has already said. If an outline never becomes a sermon, the study has not failed. Scripture has still done its work.

Pastoral Awareness Before You Preach

The goal of preaching is not only to explain a text. It is to serve people with the truth of God in the presence of God. That means the same outline can land differently depending on what your congregation is carrying: grief, conflict, shame, addiction, loneliness or burnout. The same message can be tailored to new believers who need milk, not arguments. Long time members who need repentance, not entertainment.

This is why prayer and pastoral awareness belong beside exegesis. A faithful elder asks not only, What does the text say, but also, What does my church need to hear from this text right now.

Before you move from study to proclamation, ask:

- Who is hurting in the room
- What sins are being excused in the room
- What truths are being forgotten in the room
- What hope is being resisted in the room
- What would faithfulness sound like in a loving tone

Let the Word remain central, and let love shape the delivery.

Elders and lay leaders serve the church best when they allow the Word of God to address them privately before they attempt to address others publicly. Personal Bible study guards against performance, protects against distortion, and anchors proclamation in faithfulness rather than urgency.

The foundations that follow are offered as tools of stewardship. They help structure thought, guard theological balance, and model responsible handling of Scripture. They are meant to be expanded only after prayer, adapted only with care, and used only in submission to the authority of the biblical text.

Let Scripture remain central.
Let prayer remain primary.
Let the Holy Spirit remain the true Teacher.

PART V
SERMON FOUNDATION

How This Sermon Template Was Designed

Each sermon foundation in this book follows a two-step pattern. This pattern is intentional. It reflects a conviction that Scripture must first form the servant before it is used to instruct the church.

1. Personal Bible Study
(Before Sermon Preparation)

The first section is private. It is written to slow the reader down and place them under the authority of the text before any public outline is considered.

Primary Scripture (ESV). The passage is identified clearly so that study begins with the Bible itself, not with ideas about the Bible.

Read the Passage Slowly. Simple prompts encourage repeated reading and careful noticing. This step resists hurried preparation and invites reverent listening.

Observe What the Text Says. Short bullet points model basic exegesis by focusing attention on what is actually present in the text before asking what it means or how it applies.

Identify the Central Truth. A single sentence summarizes the main idea of the passage. This trains the reader to look for the author's primary burden rather than collecting disconnected points.

Let Scripture Interpret Scripture. Related passages are provided to demonstrate how the Bible explains itself. This reinforces the historic Adventist conviction that doctrine is built from the harmony of Scripture, not isolated verses.

Personal Reflection Before God and Prayer Before Moving Forward. Questions and prayer direction invite the reader to respond personally to the passage. The goal is transformation, not merely information.

This entire first section is designed so that, even if a sermon is never preached, the study has still done its work in the life of the leader.

2. Sermon Training Outline
(For Public Teaching)

Only after personal study does the training outline appear. This section is not a manuscript. It is a framework that demonstrates how careful study becomes responsible proclamation.

Primary Biblical Text and Big Idea. These restate what has already been discovered in study, modeling sermons that grow from the central truth of the passage.

Exegetical Observations. Key details from the text are highlighted to show how structure and wording support the main idea. This models preaching that rises from the text rather than from opinion.

Scripture Interpreting Scripture. Cross references from the study section are now used publicly, demonstrating how the whole Bible speaks with a unified voice.

Christ Centered Focus. A brief statement shows how the passage leads to Christ and His saving work, guarding sermons from becoming merely moral or informational.

Adventist Theological Trajectory. A short line connects the passage to the larger Adventist message, such as sanctuary, judgment, Sabbath, or mission, helping leaders preach in a way that is both biblical and Adventist.

Sermon Movement. A simple three part flow illustrates how to organize a message clearly without scripting every word.

Pastoral Application, Prayer, and Training Notes. These elements keep preaching grounded in lived faith, dependent on the Holy Spirit, and clearly identified as training material to be expanded through prayer rather than read verbatim.

Together, these two stages train elders and lay leaders to begin with Scripture, allow the Word to address them privately, and then shape what they have received into clear, Christ centered, Adventist faithful preaching for the church.

Example: How One Sermon Foundation Was Developed

This worked example follows the exact template you just read. It demonstrates how personal study precedes public teaching, with Scripture remaining central throughout.

Personal Bible Study

(Before Sermon Preparation)

Primary Scripture (ESV)

Exodus 3:1–4:17 (Moses' call and reluctance)

1. Read the Passage Slowly

- Note God's initiative and Moses' repeated objections
- Observe what God does not say in response to Moses' inadequacy
- Pay attention to the promise that governs the entire exchange
- 2. Observe What the Text Says
- God calls from the burning bush, not from human merit
- Moses protests personal inability four times

- God responds with His presence, not reassurance of Moses' gifts
- Aaron's role is a concession, not the solution

3. Identify the Central Truth

God calls reluctant servants and promises His presence as they obey.

4. Let Scripture Interpret Scripture

- 1 Kings 19:1–18 (Elijah's collapse after faithfulness)
- Jonah 1:1–3 (Flight from divine command)
- Matthew 28:20 (Christ's promise: "I am with you always")

5. Personal Reflection Before God

- Where do I resist because the task feels beyond me?
- Do I seek God's presence more than His permission?

Prayer Before Moving Forward

Ask for courage to obey despite reluctance, trusting the promise of divine presence.

Reluctance and the Biblical Pattern of Divine Calling
Exodus 3:1–4:17 (ESV)

Introduction

Church family, have you ever felt called to serve but hesitated? Not from laziness, but from an honest awareness that God's work carries weight beyond our control. Scripture does not hide this reality. It shows leaders who resisted divine calls, not from rebellion, but from reverence. Here we see a consistent biblical pattern. God calls reluctant servants and promises His presence as they obey.

The Divine Call (Exodus 3:1–10)

Moses was not seeking promotion. At the burning bush, God initiates the encounter. "I have surely seen the affliction of my people... Come, I will send you to Pharaoh" (Exod. 3:7, 10, ESV). The text emphasizes that God reveals Himself first. The call flows from who God is, the great I AM, not from Moses' qualifications. God does not wait for readiness. He calls and then equips.

Honest Reluctance (Exodus 3:11–4:17)

Moses objects four times. "Who am I?" (Exod. 3:11, ESV). "What shall I say?" (Exod. 3:13, ESV). "They will not believe me" (Exod. 4:1, ESV). "I am slow of speech" (Exod. 4:10, ESV). These are not excuses born of rebellion, but honest expressions of fear. God does not shame Moses. He reveals His name. He grants signs. He allows Aaron's assistance. Yet the governing promise remains unchanged. "I will be with you" (Exod. 3:12, ESV). Reluctance often marks those who understand the gravity of speaking for God.

Scripture Interprets Scripture

This pattern repeats throughout Scripture. Elijah stands faithfully on Mount Carmel and then collapses under the weight of the calling, crying out, "It is enough; now, O LORD, take away my life" (1 Kings 19:4, ESV). Jonah flees toward Tarshish rather than face the burden of Nineveh's call (Jonah 1:3, ESV). God consistently calls the hesitant because He knows their frailty and chooses to walk with them anyway.

Christ Centered Promise

The assurance given to Moses, "I will be with you," finds its fullest expression in Jesus Christ, Emmanuel, God with us. At the conclusion of the Great Commission, Christ echoes the same promise. "I am with you always, to the end of the age" (Matt. 28:20, ESV). Our reluctance meets God's faithfulness in the gospel.

Adventist Echo

Early Adventist pioneers reflected this same pattern. William Miller delayed nearly nine years before publicly proclaiming his message. Ellen White often spoke of her physical frailty and hesitation. J. N. Andrews carried the heavy loneliness of mission work in Europe. Their lives remind us that ministry flows from divine mandate, not personal ambition.[41]

Pastoral Application

Elder or lay leader, if reluctance grips your heart, name it honestly. It may not disqualify you. It may confirm the seriousness with which you approach God's call. Trust not your readiness, but God's presence. Step forward where He leads. The church does not need your perfection. It needs your obedience.

Closing Prayer

Lord, call us despite our fears. Walk with us as we obey. Let Your presence overcome our reluctance. Amen.

---

[41] George R. Knight, *Millennial Fever and the End of the World* (Boise, ID: Pacific Press, 1993), 71–74; Ellen G. White, *Life Sketches* (Mountain View, CA: Pacific Press, 1915), 69–72; Benjamin L. McArthur, "J. N. Andrews: The First Missionary," *Adventist Heritage* 4, no. 1 (1977): 12–18.

Sermon Foundations by Theme (50+ Outlines)

Theme	Focus	Sermons Included	Pages
Grace Foundations	Salvation by faith	1–4, 3 (Eph 2), 6 (James 2)	120–130
Law & Obedience	Grace-motivated living	8–12, 9 (Rom 13), 10 (Jer 31)	131–145
Sabbath Rest	God's gift of rhythm	14–19, 15 (Gen 2), 18 (Luke 4)	146–155
Sanctuary Ministry	Christ as High Priest	20–21, 13 (Heb 8)	156–162
Character Formation	Christlike living	22–26, 37 (Matt 5)	163–172
Prophetic Assurance	Kingdoms & history	27–31, 27 (Dan 2)	173–182
End-Time Faithfulness	Loyalty under pressure	32–36, 32 (Rev 14), 34 (Rev 12)	183–195
Three Angels' Call	Final gospel message	35 (Rev 14:6–12)	196–200
Resurrection Hope	Victory over death	40–42, 42 (John 11)	201–210
New Creation Glory	Eternity's promise	43–52, 45 (Rev 21), 52 (Matt 24)	211–225

SERMON 1
A People of the Book
Personal Bible Study
(Before Sermon Preparation)

Primary Scripture (ESV)

2 Timothy 3:16–17

1. Read the Passage Slowly

- Note the repeated emphasis on "all Scripture"
- Observe what Scripture is said to *do*
- Pay attention to the purpose statement in verse 17

2. Observe What the Text Says

- Paul is instructing Timothy in a pastoral context
- Scripture is described as God-breathed
- Scripture is presented as sufficient for formation and service

3. Identify the Central Truth

God has given Scripture to fully equip His people for faithful living and service.

4. Let Scripture Interpret Scripture

- Psalm 119:105
- Hebrews 4:12
- John 17:17

5. Personal Reflection Before God

- Do I approach Scripture as authority or as resource?
- Am I shaped by the Word before I speak from it?

Prayer Before Moving Forward

Ask for humility, attentiveness, and submission to Scripture.

Sermon Training Outline
(For Public Teaching)

1. Primary Biblical Text (ESV)

2 Timothy 3:16–17

Paul's pastoral instruction emphasizing Scripture's divine origin and purpose.

2. Big Idea of the Text

God-breathed Scripture equips God's people for every good work.

3. Exegetical Observations

- "All Scripture" emphasizes completeness
- "Breathed out by God" establishes authority
- Fourfold usefulness leads to maturity

4. Scripture Interpreting Scripture

Psalm 119:105; Hebrews 4:12; John 17:17

5. Christ-Centered Focus

Christ is revealed through Scripture as God's saving truth.

6. Adventist Theological Trajectory

Scripture as final authority for doctrine, mission, and reform.

7. Sermon Movement

Authority of Scripture → Purpose of Scripture → Life shaped by Scripture

8. Pastoral Application

Call to faithful submission to the Word of God.

9. Prayer and the Holy Spirit

Dependence on the Spirit to teach and apply Scripture.

10. Training Notes

This outline must remain Scripture-governed and Christ-centered. Expansion should clarify the text, not replace it.

SERMON 2

The Everlasting Gospel
Revelation 14:6 (ESV)
Personal Bible Study
(Before Sermon Preparation)

Primary Scripture (ESV)

Revelation 14:6

1. Read the Passage Slowly

- Observe the scope of the proclamation
- Note the description "everlasting"

2. Observe What the Text Says

- The gospel is proclaimed globally
- It precedes judgment
- It is eternal, not situational

3. Identify the Central Truth

God's gospel message is timeless and intended for all humanity.

4. Let Scripture Interpret Scripture

Matthew 24:14; Romans 1:16

5. Personal Reflection Before God

- Is my understanding of the gospel complete or partial?
- Do I treat the gospel as urgent and hopeful?

Prayer Before Moving Forward

Ask for clarity and faithfulness in proclaiming the gospel.

Sermon Training Outline
(For Public Teaching)

1. Primary Biblical Text

Revelation 14:6 in an end-time proclamation context

2. Big Idea of the Text

The gospel remains central to God's final message.

3. Exegetical Observations

- "Everlasting" emphasizes continuity
- Global scope is explicit

4. Scripture Interpreting Scripture

Genesis 3:15; Matthew 24:14

5. Christ-Centered Focus

Christ's saving work defines the gospel.

6. Adventist Theological Trajectory

The gospel at the heart of the Three Angels' Messages.

7. Sermon Movement

Eternal gospel → Global mission → Decision

8. Pastoral Application

Proclaim Christ faithfully and clearly.

9. Prayer and the Holy Spirit

Dependence on God's power in witness.

10. Training Notes

Avoid separating gospel from obedience.

SERMON 3

Saved by Grace, Transformed by Truth

Ephesians 2:8–10 (ESV)

Personal Bible Study

(Before Sermon Preparation)

Primary Scripture (ESV)

Ephesians 2:8–10

1. Read the Passage Slowly

- Observe the contrast between grace and works
- Note the purpose of good works

2. Observe What the Text Says

- Salvation is a gift
- Good works follow salvation

3. Identify the Central Truth

Grace saves and transforms believers for faithful living.

4. Let Scripture Interpret Scripture

Titus 3:5; Romans 6:4

5. Personal Reflection Before God

- Am I trusting grace or performance?
- Does my life reflect transformation?

Prayer Before Moving Forward

Ask for gratitude and obedience rooted in grace.

Sermon Training Outline
(For Public Teaching)

1. Primary Biblical Text

Ephesians 2:8–10

2. Big Idea of the Text

Grace saves and produces obedience.

3. Exegetical Observations

- "Not of works" (Eph. 2:9) clarified by "created for good works" (Eph 2:10).

4. Scripture Interpreting Scripture

Romans 6:1–4

5. Christ-Centered Focus

Salvation accomplished through Christ alone.

6. Adventist Theological Trajectory

Justification and sanctification in harmony.

7. Sermon Movement

Grace → New identity → Obedient life

8. Pastoral Application

Live out grace faithfully.

9. Prayer and the Holy Spirit

Dependence on God's transforming power.

10. Training Notes

Never reverse the order of grace and obedience.

SERMON 4

The Character of God on Trial
Romans 3:23–26 (ESV)
Personal Bible Study
(Before Sermon Preparation)

Primary Scripture (ESV)

Romans 3:23–26

1. Read the Passage Slowly

- Note the problem of sin
- Observe how God's righteousness is demonstrated

2. Observe What the Text Says

- All have sinned
- God remains just while justifying

3. Identify the Central Truth

God's justice and mercy meet in Christ.

4. Let Scripture Interpret Scripture

Psalm 85:10; Revelation 15:3

5. Personal Reflection Before God

- Do I trust God's character fully?
- How does the cross shape my understanding of justice?

Prayer Before Moving Forward

Ask for confidence in God's righteousness.

Sermon Training Outline
(For Public Teaching)

1. Primary Biblical Text

Romans 3:23–26

2. Big Idea of the Text

God is just and merciful through Christ's sacrifice.

3. Exegetical Observations

- Righteousness demonstrated publicly
- Sin addressed without compromise

4. Scripture Interpreting Scripture

Revelation 15:3

5. Christ-Centered Focus

Christ reveals God's true character.

6. Adventist Theological Trajectory

Great Controversy theme.

7. Sermon Movement

Sin exposed → God justified → Redemption revealed

8. Pastoral Application

Trust God's justice and mercy.

9. Prayer and the Holy Spirit

Confidence in God's character.

10. Training Notes

Avoid abstract philosophy; stay cross-centered.

SERMON 5
Created in His Image
Genesis 1:26–27 (ESV)
Personal Bible Study
(Before Sermon Preparation)

Primary Scripture (ESV)

Genesis 1:26–27

1. Read the Passage Slowly

- Read the text twice, noting repetition of "image" and "likeness"
- Observe the plural language ("Let us make")
- Note the scope of humanity created male and female

2. Observe What the Text Says

- Humanity is created intentionally
- God grants representative authority
- Human identity is grounded in God's design

3. Identify the Central Truth

Human beings are created to reflect God's character and purpose.

4. Let Scripture Interpret Scripture

Psalm 8:4–6; Colossians 1:15

5. Personal Reflection Before God

- How does this passage shape my view of human worth?
- Do I reflect God's character in how I live and treat others?

Prayer Before Moving Forward

Ask God to restore His image in your life.

Sermon Training Outline
(For Public Teaching)

1. Primary Biblical Text

Genesis 1:26–27 in the creation narrative

2. Big Idea of the Text

God created humanity to reflect His character and authority.

3. Exegetical Observations

- "Image" emphasizes representation, not physical form
- Authority is given as stewardship

4. Scripture Interpreting Scripture

Psalm 8:4–6

5. Christ-Centered Focus

Christ restores the image of God in fallen humanity.

6. Adventist Theological Trajectory

Creation doctrine and human dignity

7. Sermon Movement

Creation → Identity → Responsibility

8. Pastoral Application

Live as God's representatives in the world.

9. Prayer and the Holy Spirit

Renewal of God's image through the Spirit.

10. Training Notes

Avoid speculation; stay grounded in the text.

SERMON 6

Faith That Works
James 2:17–18 (ESV)
Personal Bible Study
(Before Sermon Preparation)
Primary Scripture (ESV)

James 2:17–18

1. Read the Passage Slowly

- Observe the contrast between claim and evidence
- Note how faith and works are connected

2. Observe What the Text Says

- Faith without action is incomplete
- Works reveal genuine faith

3. Identify the Central Truth

True faith is demonstrated through obedient action.

4. Let Scripture Interpret Scripture

Matthew 7:16–20; Galatians 5:6

5. Personal Reflection Before God

- Does my faith show evidence in my life?
- Where is God calling me to active obedience?

Prayer Before Moving Forward

Ask God for living, obedient faith.

Sermon Training Outline
(For Public Teaching)

1. Primary Biblical Text

James 2:17–18 addressing practical faith

2. Big Idea of the Text

Genuine faith expresses itself through action.

3. Exegetical Observations

- Faith and works are inseparable
- Works reveal, not replace, faith

4. Scripture Interpreting Scripture

Galatians 5:6

5. Christ-Centered Focus

Christ models obedient faith.

6. Adventist Theological Trajectory

Faith and obedience held together

7. Sermon Movement

Claim → Evidence → Living faith

8. Pastoral Application

Allow faith to shape daily actions.

9. Prayer and the Holy Spirit

Dependence on God for obedient living.

10. Training Notes

Avoid legalism and passivity alike.

SERMON 7

Called by God's Name
Isaiah 43:1 (ESV)
Personal Bible Study
(Before Sermon Preparation)
Primary Scripture (ESV)

Isaiah 43:1

1. Read the Passage Slowly

- Note God's actions toward His people
- Observe the repeated assurance "fear not"

2. Observe What the Text Says

- God creates, redeems, and calls His people
- Belonging precedes command

3. Identify the Central Truth

God redeems His people and claims them as His own.

4. Let Scripture Interpret Scripture

Exodus 19:5; John 10:3

5. Personal Reflection Before God

- Do I live from my identity in God?
- Where do fear and belonging compete in my life?

Prayer Before Moving Forward

Ask God for assurance in His redeeming love.

Sermon Training Outline
(For Public Teaching)

1. Primary Biblical Text

Isaiah 43:1 in a redemption context

2. Big Idea of the Text

God calls His redeemed people by name.

3. Exegetical Observations

- Creation, redemption, and calling linked
- Fear replaced by belonging

4. Scripture Interpreting Scripture

Exodus 19:5–6

5. Christ-Centered Focus

Redemption fulfilled through Christ.

6. Adventist Theological Trajectory

Identity before mission

7. Sermon Movement

Fear → Redemption → Identity

8. Pastoral Application

Live confidently as God's people.

9. Prayer and the Holy Spirit

Assurance and trust in God.

10. Training Notes

Emphasize God's initiative, not human worth.

SERMON 8

The Law of Liberty
James 1:25 (ESV)
Personal Bible Study
(Before Sermon Preparation)
Primary Scripture (ESV)

James 1:25

1. Read the Passage Slowly

- Observe contrasts between hearing and doing
- Note the promise of blessing

2. Observe What the Text Says

- God's law brings freedom
- Obedience leads to blessing

3. Identify the Central Truth

God's law frees those who live by it.

4. Let Scripture Interpret Scripture

Psalm 119:44–45; John 8:31–32

5. Personal Reflection Before God

- Do I see obedience as burden or freedom?
- Where is God calling me to faithful action?

Prayer Before Moving Forward

Ask God for joyful obedience.

Sermon Training Outline (For Public Teaching)

1. Primary Biblical Text
James 1:25

2. Big Idea of the Text
God's law brings freedom through obedience.

3. Exegetical Observations
- "Law of liberty" unites law and freedom
- Perseverance emphasized

4. Scripture Interpreting Scripture
Psalm 119:45

5. Christ-Centered Focus
Christ teaches true freedom through obedience.

6. Adventist Theological Trajectory
Law and grace in harmony

7. Sermon Movement
Hearing → Doing → Blessing

8. Pastoral Application
Embrace obedience as freedom.

9. Prayer and the Holy Spirit
Dependence on God for faithful living.

10. Training Notes
Avoid legalistic framing.

SERMON 9

Love Is the Fulfillment of the Law
Romans 13:8–10 (ESV)
Personal Bible Study
(Before Sermon Preparation)

Primary Scripture (ESV)

Romans 13:8–10

1. Read the Passage Slowly

- Observe the repeated emphasis on love
- Note how commandments are summarized

2. Observe What the Text Says

- Love is described as an ongoing obligation
- Love causes no harm to others
- Love fulfills the law rather than replacing it

3. Identify the Central Truth

Love fulfills the law because it seeks the good of others.

4. Let Scripture Interpret Scripture

Matthew 22:37–40; Galatians 5:14

5. Personal Reflection Before God

- Does love govern my obedience?
- Where might obedience lack compassion?

Prayer Before Moving Forward

Ask God to shape obedience through love.

Sermon Training Outline
(For Public Teaching)

1. Primary Biblical Text

Romans 13:8–10 in ethical instruction

2. Big Idea of the Text

Love fulfills God's law by expressing its intent.

3. Exegetical Observations

- Commandments are relational
- Love prevents harm

4. Scripture Interpreting Scripture

Matthew 22:40

5. Christ-Centered Focus

Christ embodies self-giving love.

6. Adventist Theological Trajectory

Law motivated by love

7. Sermon Movement

Love owed → Law fulfilled → God honored

8. Pastoral Application

Let love guide obedience.

9. Prayer and the Holy Spirit

Spirit-shaped love for others.

10. Training Notes

Do not separate love from God's commands.

SERMON 10

The Law Written on the Heart
Jeremiah 31:33 (ESV)
Personal Bible Study
(Before Sermon Preparation)

Primary Scripture (ESV)

Jeremiah 31:33

1. Read the Passage Slowly

- Observe God's promise of a new covenant
- Note where the law is written

2. Observe What the Text Says

- The law remains
- The location of the law changes
- Relationship is restored

3. Identify the Central Truth

God transforms His people by internalizing His law.

4. Let Scripture Interpret Scripture

Hebrews 8:10; Ezekiel 36:26–27

5. Personal Reflection Before God

- Is obedience internal or external?
- Where is God reshaping my heart?

Prayer Before Moving Forward

Ask God for heart-level obedience.

Sermon Training Outline
(For Public Teaching)

1. Primary Biblical Text

Jeremiah 31:33

2. Big Idea of the Text

God writes His law on transformed hearts.

3. Exegetical Observations

- Covenant renewal, not abolition
- Relationship language emphasized

4. Scripture Interpreting Scripture

Hebrews 8:10

5. Christ-Centered Focus

Christ inaugurates the new covenant.

6. Adventist Theological Trajectory

Continuity of God's law

7. Sermon Movement

Broken covenant → Divine promise → Inner renewal

8. Pastoral Application

Seek obedience shaped by love.

9. Prayer and the Holy Spirit

Submission to God's transforming work.

10. Training Notes

Clarify continuity, not replacement.

SERMON 11

Obedience as Relationship
John 14:15 (ESV)
Personal Bible Study
(Before Sermon Preparation)

Primary Scripture (ESV)
John 14:15

1. Read the Passage Slowly
- Observe the conditional structure
- Note the connection between love and obedience

2. Observe What the Text Says
- Obedience flows from love
- Commands are relational, not arbitrary

3. Identify the Central Truth
Love for Christ expresses itself through obedience.

4. Let Scripture Interpret Scripture
1 John 5:3; Deuteronomy 6:5

5. Personal Reflection Before God
- What motivates my obedience?
- Where might love be growing cold?

Prayer Before Moving Forward
Ask God to deepen love for Christ.

Sermon Training Outline
(For Public Teaching)

1. Primary Biblical Text
John 14:15 in farewell discourse

2. Big Idea of the Text
Obedience flows naturally from love for Christ.

3. Exegetical Observations
- Love precedes command-keeping

4. Scripture Interpreting Scripture
1 John 5:3

5. Christ-Centered Focus
Christ invites relational faithfulness.

6. Adventist Theological Trajectory
Commandments kept through relationship

7. Sermon Movement
Love → Obedience → Abiding

8. Pastoral Application
Examine the heart behind obedience.

9. Prayer and the Holy Spirit
Love empowered by the Spirit.

10. Training Notes
Avoid moralism.

SERMON 12

Established, Not Abolished

Romans 3:31 (ESV)

Personal Bible Study

(Before Sermon Preparation)

Primary Scripture (ESV)

Romans 3:31

1. Read the Passage Slowly

- Note Paul's rhetorical question
- Observe the emphatic response

2. Observe What the Text Says

- Faith does not nullify the law
- Faith upholds God's law

3. Identify the Central Truth

True faith establishes God's law.

4. Let Scripture Interpret Scripture

Matthew 5:17; Romans 7:12

5. Personal Reflection Before God

- Do I pit faith against obedience?
- How does faith shape my loyalty to God's will?

Prayer Before Moving Forward

Ask God for doctrinal clarity and balance.

Sermon Training Outline
(For Public Teaching)

1. Primary Biblical Text

Romans 3:31

2. Big Idea of the Text

Faith upholds, rather than abolishes, God's law.

3. Exegetical Observations

- Strong negation emphasizes correction

4. Scripture Interpreting Scripture

Matthew 5:17

5. Christ-Centered Focus

Christ fulfills the law's purpose.

6. Adventist Theological Trajectory

Harmony of law and gospel

7. Sermon Movement

Misunderstanding → Clarification → Balance

8. Pastoral Application

Hold faith and obedience together.

9. Prayer and the Holy Spirit

Wisdom and humility.

10. Training Notes

Teach textually, not defensively.

SERMON 13

Walking as Jesus Walked
1 John 2:3–6 (ESV)
Personal Bible Study
(Before Sermon Preparation)

Primary Scripture (ESV)

1 John 2:3–6

1. Read the Passage Slowly

- Note the contrast between claiming and living
- Observe repeated references to knowing Christ

2. Observe What the Text Says

- Obedience confirms relationship
- Claim without practice is exposed
- Christ's life becomes the pattern

3. Identify the Central Truth

Those who truly know Christ will live as He lived.

4. Let Scripture Interpret Scripture

John 13:15; Philippians 2:5

5. Personal Reflection Before God

- Does my life align with my confession?
- Where is Christ calling me to deeper imitation?

Prayer Before Moving Forward

Ask for grace to walk faithfully as Christ walked.

Sermon Training Outline
(For Public Teaching)

1. Primary Biblical Text

1 John 2:3–6 addressing assurance of faith

2. Big Idea of the Text

Knowing Christ results in Christlike living.

3. Exegetical Observations

- Obedience verifies relationship
- "Walk" implies consistent pattern

4. Scripture Interpreting Scripture

John 13:15

5. Christ-Centered Focus

Christ is both Savior and example.

6. Adventist Theological Trajectory

Sanctification as Christ-shaped living

7. Sermon Movement

Knowing → Abiding → Walking

8. Pastoral Application

Align daily life with Christ's example.

9. Prayer and the Holy Spirit

Dependence on the Spirit for transformation.

10. Training Notes

Avoid perfectionism; emphasize grace.

SERMON 14

The Sabbath as a Gift
Mark 2:27–28 (ESV)
Personal Bible Study
(Before Sermon Preparation)

Primary Scripture (ESV)

Mark 2:27–28

1. Read the Passage Slowly

- Observe Jesus' corrective teaching
- Note the purpose statement about the Sabbath

2. Observe What the Text Says

- Sabbath was made for humanity
- Jesus claims lordship over the Sabbath

3. Identify the Central Truth

The Sabbath is God's gift, not a burden.

4. Let Scripture Interpret Scripture

Genesis 2:1–3; Exodus 20:8–11

5. Personal Reflection Before God

- How do I experience the Sabbath?
- Does it reflect rest or obligation?

Prayer Before Moving Forward

Ask God for renewed joy in Sabbath rest.

Sermon Training Outline
(For Public Teaching)

1. Primary Biblical Text

Mark 2:27–28 correcting distorted Sabbath practice

2. Big Idea of the Text

God gave the Sabbath as a blessing for humanity.

3. Exegetical Observations

- Purpose emphasized over restriction
- Authority of Christ affirmed

4. Scripture Interpreting Scripture

Genesis 2:1–3

5. Christ-Centered Focus

Christ restores the Sabbath's true meaning.

6. Adventist Theological Trajectory

Sabbath as creation gift and covenant sign

7. Sermon Movement

Misuse → Intent → Restoration

8. Pastoral Application

Receive the Sabbath as grace.

9. Prayer and the Holy Spirit

Rest and renewal through Christ.

10. Training Notes

Avoid defensive tone.

SERMON 15
Rest from Creation to Redemption
Genesis 2:1–3 (ESV)
Personal Bible Study
(Before Sermon Preparation)

Primary Scripture (ESV)

Genesis 2:1–3

1. Read the Passage Slowly

- Observe God's actions on the seventh day
- Note blessing and sanctification

2. Observe What the Text Says

- God rests, blesses, and sanctifies time
- No command is given, but a pattern is set

3. Identify the Central Truth

Sabbath rest is rooted in God's creative work.

4. Let Scripture Interpret Scripture

Hebrews 4:4; Isaiah 66:22–23

5. Personal Reflection Before God

- How does rest reflect trust in God?
- Where do I resist stopping?

Prayer Before Moving Forward

Ask God to teach trust through rest.

Sermon Training Outline

(For Public Teaching)

1. Primary Biblical Text

Genesis 2:1–3 in the creation account

2. Big Idea of the Text

God established Sabbath rest at creation.

3. Exegetical Observations

- Blessing and sanctification precede sin
- Time is set apart

4. Scripture Interpreting Scripture

Hebrews 4:4; Isaiah 66:22-23; Exodus 16:22-30

5. Christ-Centered Focus

Rest finds fullness in Christ.

6. Adventist Theological Trajectory

Creation foundation of the Sabbath

7. Sermon Movement

Creation → Blessing → Ongoing significance

8. Pastoral Application

Practice trust through rest.

9. Prayer and the Holy Spirit

Dependence on God's provision.

10. Training Notes

Anchor teaching in Scripture, not tradition.

SERMON 16

Remembering What God Remembered

Exodus 20:8–11 (ESV)

Personal Bible Study

(Before Sermon Preparation)

Primary Scripture (ESV)

Exodus 20:8–11

1. Read the Passage Slowly

- Observe the command to remember
- Note the creation rationale

2. Observe What the Text Says

- Sabbath is grounded in creation
- Rest extends to household and community

3. Identify the Central Truth

God calls His people to remember creation through Sabbath observance.

4. Let Scripture Interpret Scripture

Genesis 2:1–3; Ezekiel 20:12

5. Personal Reflection Before God

- What does Sabbath remembrance shape in me?
- How does it affect my worship and trust?

Prayer Before Moving Forward

Ask God to deepen faithful remembrance.

Sermon Training Outline
(For Public Teaching)

1. Primary Biblical Text

Exodus 20:8–11 within the Decalogue

2. Big Idea of the Text

Sabbath remembrance anchors worship in creation.

3. Exegetical Observations

- "Remember" assumes prior knowledge
- Creation reason given

4. Scripture Interpreting Scripture

Ezekiel 20:12

5. Christ-Centered Focus

Christ affirms the Sabbath's meaning.

6. Adventist Theological Trajectory

Sabbath as sign of loyalty

7. Sermon Movement

Command → Reason → Covenant sign

8. Pastoral Application

Practice intentional Sabbath remembrance.

9. Prayer and the Holy Spirit

Faithfulness in worship.

10. Training Notes

Teach command within grace.

SERMON 17

Delight in the Lord's Day
Isaiah 58:13–14 (ESV)
Personal Bible Study
(Before Sermon Preparation)

Primary Scripture (ESV)

Isaiah 58:13–14

1. Read the Passage Slowly

- Observe the contrast between self-pleasure and God's pleasure
- Note the promise attached to delight

2. Observe What the Text Says

- Sabbath observance involves intention and posture
- Delight replaces burden
- God responds with blessing

3. Identify the Central Truth

The Sabbath becomes joy when centered on God rather than self.

4. Let Scripture Interpret Scripture

Psalm 37:4; Matthew 11:28–29

5. Personal Reflection Before God

- What shapes my Sabbath experience?
- Where might self-interest replace delight in God?

Prayer Before Moving Forward

Ask God to teach joyful Sabbath keeping.

Sermon Training Outline
(For Public Teaching)

1. Primary Biblical Text

Isaiah 58:13–14 within covenant renewal

2. Big Idea of the Text

God invites His people to delight in the Sabbath.

3. Exegetical Observations

- Delight is commanded
- Promise follows obedience

4. Scripture Interpreting Scripture

Psalm 37:4

5. Christ-Centered Focus

Christ offers true rest and joy.

6. Adventist Theological Trajectory

Sabbath as relational delight

7. Sermon Movement

Misplaced focus → God-centered delight → Blessing

8. Pastoral Application

Reorient Sabbath toward joy in God.

9. Prayer and the Holy Spirit

Joyful obedience through the Spirit.

10. Training Notes

Avoid rule-centered emphasis.

SERMON 18

The Lord of the Sabbath
Luke 4:16 (ESV)
Personal Bible Study
(Before Sermon Preparation)

Primary Scripture (ESV)

Luke 4:16

1. Read the Passage Slowly

- Observe Jesus' Sabbath custom
- Note the setting of worship

2. Observe What the Text Says

- Jesus regularly worshiped on the Sabbath
- Scripture reading is central

3. Identify the Central Truth

Jesus honored the Sabbath as part of faithful worship.

4. Let Scripture Interpret Scripture

Mark 2:27–28; Hebrews 13:8

5. Personal Reflection Before God

- What habits shape my worship life?
- Does Christ's example guide my practice?

Prayer Before Moving Forward

Ask God for faithfulness in worship.

Sermon Training Outline (For Public Teaching)

1. Primary Biblical Text

Luke 4:16 describing Jesus' worship practice

2. Big Idea of the Text

Christ models faithful Sabbath observance.

3. Exegetical Observations

- "As was his custom" indicates consistency

4. Scripture Interpreting Scripture

Mark 2:28

5. Christ-Centered Focus

Christ is Lord of the Sabbath.

6. Adventist Theological Trajectory

Jesus-centered Sabbath observance

7. Sermon Movement

Practice → Authority → Example

8. Pastoral Application

Follow Christ's example in worship.

9. Prayer and the Holy Spirit

Commitment to Christlike faithfulness.

10. Training Notes

Let Christ define practice.

SERMON 19

The Sabbath and the People of God

Hebrews 4:9–10 (ESV)

Personal Bible Study

(Before Sermon Preparation)

Primary Scripture (ESV)

Hebrews 4:9–10

1. Read the Passage Slowly

- Observe the promise of rest
- Note continuity of Sabbath rest

2. Observe What the Text Says

- A Sabbath rest remains
- Rest reflects God's completed work

3. Identify the Central Truth

God invites His people into enduring rest.

4. Let Scripture Interpret Scripture

Genesis 2:2; Revelation 14:13

5. Personal Reflection Before God

- Where do I struggle to rest in God's work?
- How does Sabbath rest shape faith?

Prayer Before Moving Forward

Ask God for trust-filled rest.

Sermon Training Outline
(For Public Teaching)

1. Primary Biblical Text

Hebrews 4:9–10 in redemptive context

2. Big Idea of the Text

Sabbath rest remains for God's people.

3. Exegetical Observations

- Rest is both present and future
- God's rest is the model

4. Scripture Interpreting Scripture

Genesis 2:2

5. Christ-Centered Focus

Christ provides ultimate rest.

6. Adventist Theological Trajectory

Sabbath and salvation connected

7. Sermon Movement

Promise → Fulfillment → Hope

8. Pastoral Application

Rest in God's finished work.

9. Prayer and the Holy Spirit

Trust and peace.

10. Training Notes

Avoid speculative readings.

SERMON 20

Christ Our Great High Priest
Hebrews 4:14–16 (ESV)
Personal Bible Study
(Before Sermon Preparation)

Primary Scripture (ESV)

Hebrews 4:14–16

1. Read the Passage Slowly

- Observe Christ's role as High Priest
- Note the invitation to draw near

2. Observe What the Text Says

- Christ sympathizes with human weakness
- Access to grace is offered

3. Identify the Central Truth

Jesus intercedes compassionately for His people.

4. Let Scripture Interpret Scripture

Hebrews 7:25; Romans 8:34

5. Personal Reflection Before God

- Do I approach God with confidence or fear?
- How does Christ's ministry shape my prayer life?

Prayer Before Moving Forward

Ask for confidence rooted in Christ.

Sermon Training Outline
(For Public Teaching)

1. Primary Biblical Text

Hebrews 4:14–16

2. Big Idea of the Text

Christ's priestly ministry invites confident faith.

3. Exegetical Observations

- Sympathy rooted in shared humanity
- Invitation to approach boldly

4. Scripture Interpreting Scripture

Hebrews 7:25

5. Christ-Centered Focus

Christ intercedes continually.

6. Adventist Theological Trajectory

Heavenly sanctuary ministry

7. Sermon Movement

Great Priest → Open access → Confident faith

8. Pastoral Application

Approach God boldly through Christ.

9. Prayer and the Holy Spirit

Confidence and dependence.

10. Training Notes

Connect doctrine to assurance.

SERMON 21

From the Cross to the Throne
Hebrews 8:1–2 (ESV)
Personal Bible Study
(Before Sermon Preparation)

Primary Scripture (ESV)

Hebrews 8:1–2

1. Read the Passage Slowly

- Observe the movement from sacrifice to ministry
- Note where Christ is seated and what He is doing

2. Observe What the Text Says

- Christ is exalted
- Christ ministers in the true heavenly sanctuary
- His work continues beyond the cross

3. Identify the Central Truth

The risen Christ now ministers for His people in heaven.

4. Let Scripture Interpret Scripture

Hebrews 9:24; Daniel 7:13–14

5. Personal Reflection Before God

- Do I think of Christ's work as finished only in the past?
- How does His present ministry affect my faith?

Prayer Before Moving Forward

Thank God for Christ's ongoing work on your behalf.

Sermon Training Outline
(For Public Teaching)

1. Primary Biblical Text

Hebrews 8:1–2 emphasizing Christ's present ministry

2. Big Idea of the Text

Christ ministers as our High Priest in the heavenly sanctuary.

3. Exegetical Observations

- "The main point" signals emphasis
- Earthly sanctuary contrasted with the true one

4. Scripture Interpreting Scripture

Hebrews 9:24

5. Christ-Centered Focus

Christ reigns and intercedes for His people.

6. Adventist Theological Trajectory

Heavenly sanctuary doctrine

7. Sermon Movement

Completed sacrifice → Exalted position → Ongoing ministry

8. Pastoral Application

Live with confidence in Christ's ministry.

9. Prayer and the Holy Spirit

Assurance and trust.

10. Training Notes

Avoid speculation; stay text-centered.

SERMON 22

Judgment as Good News
Daniel 7:9–14 (ESV)
Personal Bible Study
(Before Sermon Preparation)

Primary Scripture (ESV)

Daniel 7:9–14

1. Read the Passage Slowly

- Observe the courtroom imagery
- Note the outcome of judgment

2. Observe What the Text Says

- God presides as Judge
- Judgment precedes the kingdom
- The Son of Man receives authority

3. Identify the Central Truth

God's judgment leads to the vindication of His people.

4. Let Scripture Interpret Scripture

Ecclesiastes 12:14; Revelation 14:7

5. Personal Reflection Before God

- Do I fear judgment or trust God's justice?
- How does this passage shape hope?

Prayer Before Moving Forward

Ask God for trust in His righteous judgment.

Sermon Training Outline
(For Public Teaching)

1. Primary Biblical Text

Daniel 7:9–14 in prophetic context

2. Big Idea of the Text

God's judgment restores justice and hope.

3. Exegetical Observations
- Judgment scene precedes kingdom transfer
- Authority given to the Son of Man

4. Scripture Interpreting Scripture

Revelation 14:7

5. Christ-Centered Focus

Christ receives the everlasting kingdom.

6. Adventist Theological Trajectory

Pre-Advent judgment as good news

7. Sermon Movement

Oppression → Judgment → Kingdom

8. Pastoral Application

Live faithfully before a just God.

9. Prayer and the Holy Spirit

Confidence in God's justice.

10. Training Notes

Avoid fear-based framing.

SERMON 23

Cleansing and Restoration
Leviticus 16:30 (ESV)
Personal Bible Study
(Before Sermon Preparation)

Primary Scripture (ESV)

Leviticus 16:30

1. Read the Passage Slowly

- Observe the purpose of the Day of Atonement
- Note the promise of cleansing

2. Observe What the Text Says

- Cleansing is God's provision
- Restoration is relational

3. Identify the Central Truth

God provides cleansing so His people may dwell with Him.

4. Let Scripture Interpret Scripture

Psalm 51:7; Hebrews 9:23

5. Personal Reflection Before God

- Where do I need God's cleansing?
- Do I trust God's provision for restoration?

Prayer Before Moving Forward

Ask for repentance and renewal.

Sermon Training Outline (For Public Teaching)

1. Primary Biblical Text

Leviticus 16:30 in sanctuary context

2. Big Idea of the Text

God cleanses His people to restore relationship.

3. Exegetical Observations

- Cleansing precedes renewed fellowship
- God acts on behalf of the people

4. Scripture Interpreting Scripture

Hebrews 9:23

5. Christ-Centered Focus

Christ fulfills atonement typology.

6. Adventist Theological Trajectory

Sanctuary cleansing theme

7. Sermon Movement

Sin → Atonement → Restoration

8. Pastoral Application

Seek God's cleansing with humility.

9. Prayer and the Holy Spirit

Repentance and renewal.

10. Training Notes

Explain typology carefully.

SERMON 24

Our Advocate with the Father
1 John 2:1–2 (ESV)
Personal Bible Study
(Before Sermon Preparation)

Primary Scripture (ESV)

1 John 2:1–2

1. Read the Passage Slowly
- Observe the balance between warning and assurance
- Note Christ's role as Advocate

2. Observe What the Text Says
- Sin is acknowledged honestly
- Christ intercedes for believers

3. Identify the Central Truth
Christ advocates for believers when they fall.

4. Let Scripture Interpret Scripture
Romans 8:1; Hebrews 7:25

5. Personal Reflection Before God
- How do I respond when I sin?
- Do I trust Christ's advocacy?

Prayer Before Moving Forward
Thank God for Christ's intercession.

Sermon Training Outline
(For Public Teaching)

1. Primary Biblical Text

1 John 2:1–2 addressing assurance

2. Big Idea of the Text

Christ intercedes faithfully for His people.

3. Exegetical Observations

- Advocacy grounded in righteousness
- Atonement sufficient for all

4. Scripture Interpreting Scripture

Hebrews 7:25

5. Christ-Centered Focus

Christ as righteous Advocate.

6. Adventist Theological Trajectory

Ongoing priestly ministry

7. Sermon Movement

Sin acknowledged → Advocate provided → Assurance

8. Pastoral Application

Come honestly before God.

9. Prayer and the Holy Spirit

Assurance of forgiveness.

10. Training Notes

Avoid minimizing sin or grace.

SERMON 25

Confidence in Christ's Ministry
Hebrews 10:19–22 (ESV)
Personal Bible Study
(Before Sermon Preparation)

Primary Scripture (ESV)

Hebrews 10:19–22

1. Read the Passage Slowly

- Observe the invitation to draw near
- Note the basis for confidence

2. Observe What the Text Says

- Access to God is granted through Christ
- Confidence rests on Christ's work, not ours

3. Identify the Central Truth

Believers may approach God confidently because of Christ.

4. Let Scripture Interpret Scripture

Hebrews 4:16; Ephesians 3:12

5. Personal Reflection Before God

- Do I approach God with confidence or hesitation?
- What grounds my assurance?

Prayer Before Moving Forward

Thank God for open access through Christ.

Sermon Training Outline
(For Public Teaching)

1. Primary Biblical Text

Hebrews 10:19–22

2. Big Idea of the Text

Christ's sacrifice provides confident access to God.

3. Exegetical Observations

- "New and living way" emphasizes access
- Hearts cleansed, bodies washed

4. Scripture Interpreting Scripture

Hebrews 4:16

5. Christ-Centered Focus

Christ opens the way into God's presence.

6. Adventist Theological Trajectory

Assurance grounded in Christ's ministry

7. Sermon Movement

Barrier removed → Access granted → Faithful approach

8. Pastoral Application

Draw near with sincerity and faith.

9. Prayer and the Holy Spirit

Bold yet reverent trust.

10. Training Notes

Balance confidence with reverence.

SERMON 26

The God Who Rules History
Daniel 2:20–22 (ESV)
Personal Bible Study
(Before Sermon Preparation)

Primary Scripture (ESV)

Daniel 2:20–22

1. Read the Passage Slowly

- Observe Daniel's praise
- Note God's control over times and rulers

2. Observe What the Text Says

- God reveals mysteries
- God removes and establishes kings

3. Identify the Central Truth

God sovereignly directs history and human affairs.

4. Let Scripture Interpret Scripture

Isaiah 46:9–10; Acts 17:26

5. Personal Reflection Before God

- Where do I struggle to trust God's sovereignty?
- How does this passage encourage faith?

Prayer Before Moving Forward

Praise God for His wisdom and control.

Sermon Training Outline
(For Public Teaching)

1. Primary Biblical Text
Daniel 2:20–22

2. Big Idea of the Text
God rules over history with wisdom and authority.

3. Exegetical Observations
- Wisdom and power belong to God
- History is not random

4. Scripture Interpreting Scripture
Isaiah 46:10

5. Christ-Centered Focus
God's rule fulfilled in Christ's kingdom.

6. Adventist Theological Trajectory
Prophetic confidence

7. Sermon Movement
Human uncertainty → Divine sovereignty → Confidence

8. Pastoral Application
Trust God amid global instability.

9. Prayer and the Holy Spirit
Confidence and peace.

10. Training Notes
Avoid speculation or date-setting.

SERMON 27

Kingdoms Rise and Fall
Daniel 2:44 (ESV)
Personal Bible Study
(Before Sermon Preparation)

Primary Scripture (ESV)

Daniel 2:44

1. Read the Passage Slowly

- Observe contrast between human kingdoms and God's kingdom
- Note permanence

2. Observe What the Text Says

- God establishes His kingdom
- Earthly kingdoms pass away

3. Identify the Central Truth

God's kingdom alone is eternal.

4. Let Scripture Interpret Scripture

Psalm 145:13; Revelation 11:15

5. Personal Reflection Before God

- Where do I place ultimate hope?
- How does this shape loyalty?

Prayer Before Moving Forward

Ask God to fix your hope on His kingdom.

Sermon Training Outline
(For Public Teaching)

1. Primary Biblical Text

Daniel 2:44

2. Big Idea of the Text

God alone establishes an everlasting kingdom.

3. Exegetical Observations

- Divine initiative emphasized
- Permanence contrasted with fragility

4. Scripture Interpreting Scripture

Revelation 11:15

5. Christ-Centered Focus

Christ reigns as eternal King.

6. Adventist Theological Trajectory

Prophetic assurance

7. Sermon Movement

Human kingdoms → Divine kingdom → Eternal hope

8. Pastoral Application

Live as citizens of God's kingdom.

9. Prayer and the Holy Spirit

Hope rooted in God's reign.

10. Training Notes

Avoid political alignment.

SERMON 28

The Sure Word of Prophecy
2 Peter 1:19 (ESV)
Personal Bible Study
(Before Sermon Preparation)

Primary Scripture (ESV)

2 Peter 1:19

1. Read the Passage Slowly

- Observe imagery of light and darkness
- Note the purpose of prophecy

2. Observe What the Text Says

- Prophecy guides believers
- Its authority is affirmed

3. Identify the Central Truth

Prophecy provides trustworthy guidance until Christ returns.

4. Let Scripture Interpret Scripture

Isaiah 46:10; Revelation 19:10

5. Personal Reflection Before God

- How do I approach prophecy?
- Does it lead me to hope and faithfulness?

Prayer Before Moving Forward

Ask God for discernment and humility.

Sermon Training Outline
(For Public Teaching)

1. Primary Biblical Text
2 Peter 1:19

2. Big Idea of the Text
Prophecy is a reliable guide for God's people.

3. Exegetical Observations
- Lamp imagery emphasizes guidance
- Fulfillment anticipated

4. Scripture Interpreting Scripture
Revelation 19:10

5. Christ-Centered Focus
Prophecy points toward Christ.

6. Adventist Theological Trajectory
Confidence in prophetic Scripture

7. Sermon Movement
Darkness → Prophetic light → Hope

8. Pastoral Application
Study prophecy with faith and humility.

9. Prayer and the Holy Spirit
Discernment and clarity.

10. Training Notes
Resist sensationalism.

SERMON 29

The Conflict Behind the Scenes

Revelation 12:7–12 (ESV)

Personal Bible Study

(Before Sermon Preparation)

Primary Scripture (ESV)

Revelation 12:7–12

1. Read the Passage Slowly

- Observe the movement from conflict to victory
- Note the perspective shift from heaven to earth

2. Observe What the Text Says

- A real spiritual conflict exists
- Satan is defeated but still active
- Christ's victory is decisive

3. Identify the Central Truth

Earthly suffering reflects a larger spiritual conflict already decided by Christ.

4. Let Scripture Interpret Scripture

Job 1:6–12; John 12:31

5. Personal Reflection Before God

- How does this passage shape my view of trials?
- Do I live from Christ's victory or from fear?

Prayer Before Moving Forward

Thank God for Christ's decisive victory.

Sermon Training Outline
(For Public Teaching)

1. Primary Biblical Text

Revelation 12:7–12 in cosmic conflict context

2. Big Idea of the Text

Christ has won the conflict, though the struggle continues briefly.

3. Exegetical Observations

- Victory declared before final removal
- Limited time emphasized

4. Scripture Interpreting Scripture

John 12:31

5. Christ-Centered Focus

Christ triumphs over Satan.

6. Adventist Theological Trajectory

Great Controversy framework

7. Sermon Movement

Conflict → Victory → Urgency

8. Pastoral Application

Stand firm in Christ's victory.

9. Prayer and the Holy Spirit

Confidence and courage.

10. Training Notes

Avoid fear-driven teaching.

SERMON 30

Babylon: Confusion and Call
Revelation 18:1–4 (ESV)
Personal Bible Study
(Before Sermon Preparation)

Primary Scripture (ESV)

Revelation 18:1–4

1. Read the Passage Slowly

- Observe God's call to separation
- Note the reason for the call

2. Observe What the Text Says

- Babylon is characterized by deception
- God calls His people out

3. Identify the Central Truth

God calls His people out of spiritual confusion into faithfulness.

4. Let Scripture Interpret Scripture

Jeremiah 51:6; 2 Corinthians 6:17

5. Personal Reflection Before God

- Where might compromise exist in my life?
- How does loyalty to God shape my choices?

Prayer Before Moving Forward

Ask for courage to follow truth.

Sermon Training Outline
(For Public Teaching)

1. Primary Biblical Text

Revelation 18:1–4

2. Big Idea of the Text

God calls His people to leave spiritual deception.

3. Exegetical Observations

- Divine authority emphasized
- Call is urgent and personal

4. Scripture Interpreting Scripture

2 Corinthians 6:17

5. Christ-Centered Focus

Christ leads His people into truth.

6. Adventist Theological Trajectory

End-time call to faithfulness

7. Sermon Movement

Deception revealed → Call issued → Faithful response

8. Pastoral Application

Choose loyalty to God's Word.

9. Prayer and the Holy Spirit

Courage and discernment.

10. Training Notes

Emphasize principles, not institutions.

SERMON 31

Worship in the Last Days
Revelation 14:7 (ESV)
Personal Bible Study
(Before Sermon Preparation)

Primary Scripture (ESV)

Revelation 14:7

1. Read the Passage Slowly

- Observe the call to worship
- Note creation language

2. Observe What the Text Says

- Worship is commanded
- Creator identity emphasized

3. Identify the Central Truth

True worship honors God as Creator and Judge.

4. Let Scripture Interpret Scripture

Exodus 20:11; John 4:23–24

5. Personal Reflection Before God

- Whom do I worship in practice?
- Does my worship honor God as Creator?

Prayer Before Moving Forward

Ask God for reverent, faithful worship.

Sermon Training Outline
(For Public Teaching)

1. Primary Biblical Text

Revelation 14:7

2. Big Idea of the Text

God calls humanity to worship Him as Creator.

3. Exegetical Observations

- Judgment and worship connected
- Creation emphasized

4. Scripture Interpreting Scripture

Exodus 20:11

5. Christ-Centered Focus

Christ restores true worship.

6. Adventist Theological Trajectory

Creation-based worship and Sabbath

7. Sermon Movement

Judgment announced → Worship commanded → Creator honored

8. Pastoral Application

Examine worship priorities.

9. Prayer and the Holy Spirit

Reverence and faithfulness.

10. Training Notes

Avoid worship-style debates.

SERMON 32
The Faith of Jesus
Revelation 14:12 (ESV)
Personal Bible Study
(Before Sermon Preparation)

Primary Scripture (ESV)

Revelation 14:12

1. Read the Passage Slowly

- Observe the description of the saints
- Note patience, obedience, and faith

2. Observe What the Text Says

- Endurance is required
- Faith and obedience are united

3. Identify the Central Truth

God's people endure through obedience and faith in Jesus.

4. Let Scripture Interpret Scripture

Galatians 2:20; Hebrews 12:2

5. Personal Reflection Before God

- Where is endurance required in my life?
- Do I rely on Christ's faithfulness?

Prayer Before Moving Forward

Ask God for enduring faith.

Sermon Training Outline
(For Public Teaching)

1. Primary Biblical Text
Revelation 14:12

2. Big Idea of the Text
Faithful endurance marks God's people.

3. Exegetical Observations
- Patience linked to obedience
- Faith centered on Jesus

4. Scripture Interpreting Scripture
Hebrews 12:2

5. Christ-Centered Focus
Jesus is the source and model of faith.

6. Adventist Theological Trajectory
End-time character development

7. Sermon Movement
Crisis → Endurance → Faithfulness

8. Pastoral Application
Remain faithful under pressure.

9. Prayer and the Holy Spirit
Strength and perseverance.

10. Training Notes
Stress grace-enabled obedience.

SERMON 33

Called Out to Be Sent
Matthew 28:18–20 (ESV)
Personal Bible Study
(Before Sermon Preparation)

Primary Scripture (ESV)

Matthew 28:18–20

1. Read the Passage Slowly

- Observe the authority claimed by Jesus
- Note the sequence of command, not just the task

2. Observe What the Text Says

- Authority precedes mission
- Making disciples involves teaching and obedience
- Christ promises His presence

3. Identify the Central Truth

Christ sends His followers to make disciples under His authority.

4. Let Scripture Interpret Scripture

Acts 1:8; John 20:21

5. Personal Reflection Before God

- How does Christ's authority shape my witness?
- Where is God sending me?

Prayer Before Moving Forward

Ask God for faithfulness in mission.

Sermon Training Outline
(For Public Teaching)

1. Primary Biblical Text

Matthew 28:18–20

2. Big Idea of the Text

The risen Christ commissions His church for mission.

3. Exegetical Observations

- Authority frames the command
- Teaching obedience emphasized

4. Scripture Interpreting Scripture

Acts 1:8

5. Christ-Centered Focus

Christ sends and sustains His people.

6. Adventist Theological Trajectory

Global mission mandate

7. Sermon Movement

Authority → Commission → Presence

8. Pastoral Application

Participate faithfully in Christ's mission.

9. Prayer and the Holy Spirit

Empowerment for witness.

10. Training Notes

Focus on discipleship, not programs.

SERMON 34

A People with a Message
Revelation 12:17 (ESV)
Personal Bible Study
(Before Sermon Preparation)

Primary Scripture (ESV)

Revelation 12:17

1. Read the Passage Slowly

- Observe the identity of God's remnant
- Note the dragon's response

2. Observe What the Text Says

- God's people keep commandments
- They hold to Jesus' testimony

3. Identify the Central Truth

God has a faithful people who remain loyal under pressure.

4. Let Scripture Interpret Scripture

Revelation 14:12; John 16:33

5. Personal Reflection Before God

- What does loyalty to God look like today?
- Where is faith tested?

Prayer Before Moving Forward

Ask God for steadfast faithfulness.

Sermon Training Outline
(For Public Teaching)

1. Primary Biblical Text
Revelation 12:17

2. Big Idea of the Text
God's people remain faithful amid opposition.

3. Exegetical Observations
- Obedience and testimony held together
- Conflict context emphasized

4. Scripture Interpreting Scripture
Revelation 14:12

5. Christ-Centered Focus
Faithfulness sustained through Christ.

6. Adventist Theological Trajectory
Remnant identity

7. Sermon Movement
Conflict → Identity → Faithfulness

8. Pastoral Application
Remain loyal to God's truth.

9. Prayer and the Holy Spirit
Courage and endurance.

10. Training Notes
Avoid triumphalism.

SERMON 35

The Three Angels' Messages
Revelation 14:6–12 (ESV)
Personal Bible Study
(Before Sermon Preparation)

Primary Scripture (ESV)

Revelation 14:6–12

1. Read the Passage Slowly

- Observe the progression of messages
- Note the repeated call to decision

2. Observe What the Text Says

- Gospel proclaimed
- Judgment announced
- Loyalty tested

3. Identify the Central Truth

God issues a final call to faithfulness through the everlasting gospel.

4. Let Scripture Interpret Scripture

Matthew 24:14; Revelation 18:1–4

5. Personal Reflection Before God

- How do these messages shape my priorities?
- Do they lead me to humility or fear?

Prayer Before Moving Forward

Ask for wisdom and balance.

Sermon Training Outline
(For Public Teaching)

1. Primary Biblical Text
Revelation 14:6–12

2. Big Idea of the Text
God's final message calls for faithful allegiance.

3. Exegetical Observations
- Messages build progressively
- Gospel remains central

4. Scripture Interpreting Scripture
Revelation 18:1–4

5. Christ-Centered Focus
Christ is central to God's final call.

6. Adventist Theological Trajectory
Three Angels' Messages as mission framework

7. Sermon Movement
Gospel → Warning → Decision

8. Pastoral Application
Respond with faith and obedience.

9. Prayer and the Holy Spirit
Clarity and courage.

10. Training Notes
Avoid sensational emphasis.

SERMON 36

Living the Truth We Proclaim
Titus 2:11–14 (ESV)
Personal Bible Study
(Before Sermon Preparation)

Primary Scripture (ESV)

Titus 2:11–14

1. Read the Passage Slowly

- Observe grace as teacher
- Note transformation and purpose

2. Observe What the Text Says

- Grace trains believers
- Redemption leads to zeal

3. Identify the Central Truth

God's grace transforms believers into faithful witnesses.

4. Let Scripture Interpret Scripture

Romans 6:1–4; James 1:22

5. Personal Reflection Before God

- Is grace shaping my daily conduct?
- Do my actions align with my confession?

Prayer Before Moving Forward

Ask God for a life shaped by grace.

Sermon Training Outline
(For Public Teaching)

1. Primary Biblical Text

Titus 2:11–14

2. Big Idea of the Text

Grace produces godly living.

3. Exegetical Observations

- Grace instructs, not excuses
- Redemption results in zeal

4. Scripture Interpreting Scripture

James 1:22

5. Christ-Centered Focus

Christ redeems and purifies His people.

6. Adventist Theological Trajectory

Holistic discipleship

7. Sermon Movement

Grace revealed → Life transformed → Hope anticipated

8. Pastoral Application

Live consistently with the gospel.

9. Prayer and the Holy Spirit

Transformation and integrity.

10. Training Notes

Avoid behavior-only emphasis.

SERMON 37

Light in a Dark World
Matthew 5:14–16 (ESV)
Personal Bible Study
(Before Sermon Preparation)

Primary Scripture (ESV)

Matthew 5:14–16

1. Read the Passage Slowly

- Observe the metaphors Jesus uses
- Note the purpose of light

2. Observe What the Text Says

- Disciples are described as light
- Light is meant to be visible
- God is glorified through visible faithfulness

3. Identify the Central Truth

God calls His people to reflect His character publicly.

4. Let Scripture Interpret Scripture

Isaiah 60:1–3; Philippians 2:15

5. Personal Reflection Before God

- Where does my faith become visible?
- Where do I hide what God has done?

Prayer Before Moving Forward

Ask God for courage to reflect His light.

Sermon Training Outline
(For Public Teaching)

1. Primary Biblical Text
Matthew 5:14–16 in the Sermon on the Mount

2. Big Idea of the Text
God's people are called to visibly reflect His light.

3. Exegetical Observations
- Identity stated before command
- Purpose is God's glory

4. Scripture Interpreting Scripture
Isaiah 60:1

5. Christ-Centered Focus
Christ is the true light reflected through His followers.

6. Adventist Theological Trajectory
Witness through character

7. Sermon Movement
Identity → Visibility → God glorified

8. Pastoral Application
Live faithfully where God has placed you.

9. Prayer and the Holy Spirit
Boldness and faithfulness.

10. Training Notes
Avoid performance-driven witness.

SERMON 38

Faithful unto Death
Revelation 2:10 (ESV)
Personal Bible Study
(Before Sermon Preparation)

Primary Scripture (ESV)

Revelation 2:10

1. Read the Passage Slowly

- Observe the encouragement amid suffering
- Note the promise attached to faithfulness

2. Observe What the Text Says

- Suffering is acknowledged
- Faithfulness is required
- Eternal reward is promised

3. Identify the Central Truth

God calls His people to faithfulness even in suffering.

4. Let Scripture Interpret Scripture

Matthew 24:13; James 1:12

5. Personal Reflection Before God

- Where is faith tested in my life?
- What sustains endurance?

Prayer Before Moving Forward

Ask God for perseverance and trust.

Sermon Training Outline
(For Public Teaching)

1. Primary Biblical Text

Revelation 2:10 addressing persecuted believers

2. Big Idea of the Text

Faithfulness unto death leads to eternal life.

3. Exegetical Observations

- Limited suffering timeframe
- Reward assured

4. Scripture Interpreting Scripture

James 1:12

5. Christ-Centered Focus

Christ remained faithful unto death.

6. Adventist Theological Trajectory

Endurance in last-day faithfulness

7. Sermon Movement

Trial → Faithfulness → Reward

8. Pastoral Application

Remain faithful under pressure.

9. Prayer and the Holy Spirit

Strength and hope.

10. Training Notes

Avoid glorifying suffering.

SERMON 39

The Blessed Hope
Titus 2:13 (ESV)
Personal Bible Study
(Before Sermon Preparation)

Primary Scripture (ESV)

Titus 2:13

1. Read the Passage Slowly

- Observe what believers await
- Note Christ's identity

2. Observe What the Text Says

- Hope is future-oriented
- Christ's return is glorious

3. Identify the Central Truth

The return of Christ is the believer's ultimate hope.

4. Let Scripture Interpret Scripture

John 14:1–3; 1 Thessalonians 4:16–17

5. Personal Reflection Before God

- How does hope shape daily living?
- Do I live expectantly?

Prayer Before Moving Forward

Ask God to renew hope and anticipation.

Sermon Training Outline
(For Public Teaching)

1. Primary Biblical Text

Titus 2:13

2. Big Idea of the Text

Christ's return anchors Christian hope.

3. Exegetical Observations

- Hope linked to appearing
- Glory emphasized

4. Scripture Interpreting Scripture

John 14:3

5. Christ-Centered Focus

Christ is the object of hope.

6. Adventist Theological Trajectory

Second Coming hope

7. Sermon Movement

Present waiting → Future appearing → Enduring hope

8. Pastoral Application

Live in light of Christ's return.

9. Prayer and the Holy Spirit

Hope and perseverance.

10. Training Notes

Avoid speculative timelines.

SERMON 40

Comfort Concerning the Dead
1 Thessalonians 4:13–18 (ESV)
Personal Bible Study
(Before Sermon Preparation)

Primary Scripture (ESV)

1 Thessalonians 4:13–18

1. Read the Passage Slowly

- Observe the pastoral tone
- Note the sequence of events

2. Observe What the Text Says

- Death is described as sleep
- Resurrection is promised
- Hope replaces grief

3. Identify the Central Truth

Believers grieve with hope because of the resurrection.

4. Let Scripture Interpret Scripture

John 11:11–14; 1 Corinthians 15:51–54

5. Personal Reflection Before God

- How does resurrection hope affect grief?
- Do I comfort others with this hope?

Prayer Before Moving Forward

Ask God to anchor hope in His promises.

Sermon Training Outline
(For Public Teaching)

1. Primary Biblical Text

1 Thessalonians 4:13–18

2. Big Idea of the Text

Resurrection hope comforts believers.

3. Exegetical Observations

- Sleep metaphor emphasized
- Sequence guards against confusion

4. Scripture Interpreting Scripture

1 Corinthians 15:52

5. Christ-Centered Focus

Christ's resurrection guarantees ours.

6. Adventist Theological Trajectory

Biblical teaching on death and resurrection

7. Sermon Movement

Grief → Promise → Comfort

8. Pastoral Application

Comfort one another with hope.

9. Prayer and the Holy Spirit

Peace and assurance.

10. Training Notes

Speak gently and pastorally.

SERMON 41

Death, the Last Enemy
1 Corinthians 15:26 (ESV)
Personal Bible Study
(Before Sermon Preparation)

Primary Scripture (ESV)

1 Corinthians 15:26

1. Read the Passage Slowly

- Observe how death is described
- Note the certainty of its destruction

2. Observe What the Text Says

- Death is an enemy
- Its defeat is future but assured

3. Identify the Central Truth

God will ultimately destroy death through Christ.

4. Let Scripture Interpret Scripture

Isaiah 25:8; Revelation 21:4

5. Personal Reflection Before God

- How does this promise shape present hope?
- Where does fear of death linger?

Prayer Before Moving Forward

Thank God for victory over death.

Sermon Training Outline
(For Public Teaching)

1. Primary Biblical Text

1 Corinthians 15:26 in resurrection teaching

2. Big Idea of the Text

Death will be fully defeated by God.

3. Exegetical Observations

- Enemy language emphasizes opposition
- Destruction is decisive

4. Scripture Interpreting Scripture

Isaiah 25:8

5. Christ-Centered Focus

Christ conquers death through resurrection.

6. Adventist Theological Trajectory

Victory over death at Christ's return

7. Sermon Movement

Enemy identified → Victory assured → Hope sustained

8. Pastoral Application

Live without fear of death.

9. Prayer and the Holy Spirit

Confidence and peace.

10. Training Notes

Avoid sentimentalizing death.

SERMON 42

The Resurrection Hope
John 11:25–26 (ESV)
Personal Bible Study
(Before Sermon Preparation)

Primary Scripture (ESV)

John 11:25–26

1. Read the Passage Slowly

- Observe Jesus' self-declaration
- Note belief and life connection

2. Observe What the Text Says

- Jesus is resurrection and life
- Faith transcends death

3. Identify the Central Truth

Life is found in Christ, even beyond death.

4. Let Scripture Interpret Scripture

1 Corinthians 15:20–22

5. Personal Reflection Before God

- Do I trust Christ fully with life and death?

Prayer Before Moving Forward

Renew faith in Christ's promise.

Sermon Training Outline
(For Public Teaching)

1. Primary Biblical Text
John 11:25–26

2. Big Idea of the Text
Jesus is the source of resurrection life.

3. Exegetical Observations
- "I am" statement central
- Faith emphasized

4. Scripture Interpreting Scripture
1 Corinthians 15:22

5. Christ-Centered Focus
Christ embodies resurrection hope.

6. Adventist Theological Trajectory
Resurrection at the Second Coming

7. Sermon Movement
Loss → Revelation → Hope

8. Pastoral Application
Trust Christ in life and death.

9. Prayer and the Holy Spirit
Hope and assurance.

10. Training Notes
Keep Christ central.

SERMON 43

The Millennium
Revelation 20:1–6 (ESV)
Personal Bible Study
(Before Sermon Preparation)

Primary Scripture (ESV)
Revelation 20:1–6

1. Read the Passage Slowly
- Observe sequence and timeframe
- Note who reigns

2. Observe What the Text Says
- Satan bound
- Saints reign with Christ

3. Identify the Central Truth
God secures justice and restoration through His plan.

4. Let Scripture Interpret Scripture
Jeremiah 4:23–26; 1 Corinthians 6:2

5. Personal Reflection Before God
- How does God's justice reassure me?

Prayer Before Moving Forward
Trust God's righteous judgment.

Sermon Training Outline
(For Public Teaching)

1. Primary Biblical Text

Revelation 20:1–6

2. Big Idea of the Text

God's plan includes restoration and justice.

3. Exegetical Observations

- Time-bound reign
- Vindication emphasized

4. Scripture Interpreting Scripture

1 Corinthians 6:2

5. Christ-Centered Focus

Christ reigns as victorious King.

6. Adventist Theological Trajectory

Millennial judgment understanding

7. Sermon Movement

Defeat of evil → Reign → Restoration

8. Pastoral Application

Trust God's justice.

9. Prayer and the Holy Spirit

Confidence in God's plan.

10. Training Notes

Avoid speculation.

SERMON 44

The End of Sin
Nahum 1:9 (ESV)
Personal Bible Study
(Before Sermon Preparation)

Primary Scripture (ESV)

Nahum 1:9

1. Read the Passage Slowly

- Observe finality language

2. Observe What the Text Says

- Sin will not rise again

3. Identify the Central Truth

God permanently eradicates evil.

4. Let Scripture Interpret Scripture

Revelation 21:4; Malachi 4:1

5. Personal Reflection Before God

- How does final justice affect hope?

Prayer Before Moving Forward

Praise God for final restoration.

Sermon Training Outline
(For Public Teaching)

1. Primary Biblical Text
Nahum 1:9

2. Big Idea of the Text
God ends sin permanently.

3. Exegetical Observations
- Finality emphasized

4. Scripture Interpreting Scripture
Revelation 21:4

5. Christ-Centered Focus
Christ secures final victory.

6. Adventist Theological Trajectory
Eradication of sin

7. Sermon Movement
Evil judged → Sin ended → Peace restored

8. Pastoral Application
Live in hope and faithfulness.

9. Prayer and the Holy Spirit
Thanksgiving and assurance.

10. Training Notes
Avoid harsh tone.

SERMON 45

Behold, I Make All Things New
Revelation 21:1–5 (ESV)
Personal Bible Study
(Before Sermon Preparation)

Primary Scripture (ESV)
Revelation 21:1–5

1. Read the Passage Slowly

- Observe renewal language

2. Observe What the Text Says

- God creates anew
- Pain is removed

3. Identify the Central Truth

God restores creation completely.

4. Let Scripture Interpret Scripture

Isaiah 65:17

5. Personal Reflection Before God

- How does restoration shape present hope?

Prayer Before Moving Forward
Thank God for renewal.

Sermon Training Outline
(For Public Teaching)

1. Primary Biblical Text

Revelation 21:1–5

2. Big Idea of the Text

God renews all things.

3. Exegetical Observations

- Divine initiative emphasized

4. Scripture Interpreting Scripture

Isaiah 65:17

5. Christ-Centered Focus

Christ restores creation.

6. Adventist Theological Trajectory

New earth hope

7. Sermon Movement

Old passes → New created → Hope fulfilled

8. Pastoral Application

Live with renewed hope.

9. Prayer and the Holy Spirit

Joy and anticipation.

10. Training Notes

Avoid escapism.

SERMON 46

God with His People
Revelation 21:3 (ESV)
Personal Bible Study
(Before Sermon Preparation)

Primary Scripture (ESV)
Revelation 21:3

1. Read the Passage Slowly
- Observe the announcement from heaven
- Note the language of dwelling and relationship

2. Observe What the Text Says
- God initiates restored relationship
- Separation caused by sin is removed
- God's presence defines the new reality

3. Identify the Central Truth
God's ultimate purpose is to dwell fully and permanently with
His people.

4. Let Scripture Interpret Scripture
Leviticus 26:11–12; John 1:14

5. Personal Reflection Before God
- How does God's presence shape my hope?
- Do I long more for God Himself than for His gifts?

Prayer Before Moving Forward
Thank God for the promise of restored fellowship.

Sermon Training Outline
(For Public Teaching)

1. Primary Biblical Text

Revelation 21:3 in the new creation vision

2. Big Idea of the Text

God restores creation by dwelling with His people.

3. Exegetical Observations
- "Dwelling place" echoes sanctuary language
- Relationship language emphasized

4. Scripture Interpreting Scripture

John 1:14; Leviticus 26:12

5. Christ-Centered Focus

Christ makes God's dwelling with humanity possible.

6. Adventist Theological Trajectory

Sanctuary fulfilled in restored relationship

7. Sermon Movement

Separation → Promise → Permanent presence

8. Pastoral Application

Live now in anticipation of God's presence.

9. Prayer and the Holy Spirit

Longing for restored fellowship.

10. Training Notes

Keep focus on relationship, not speculation.

SERMON 47

Even So, Come, Lord Jesus
Revelation 22:20 (ESV)
Personal Bible Study
(Before Sermon Preparation)

Primary Scripture (ESV)

Revelation 22:20

1. Read the Passage Slowly

- Observe the dialogue between Christ and the church
- Note the tone of longing

2. Observe What the Text Says

- Christ promises His return
- The church responds with longing

3. Identify the Central Truth

The faithful church longs for Christ's return.

4. Let Scripture Interpret Scripture

1 Corinthians 16:22; Titus 2:13

5. Personal Reflection Before God

- Do I truly desire Christ's return?
- How does hope shape my daily life?

Prayer Before Moving Forward

Ask God to deepen longing for Christ's appearing.

Sermon Training Outline
(For Public Teaching)

1. Primary Biblical Text

Revelation 22:20 concluding Scripture

2. Big Idea of the Text

Hope in Christ's return shapes faithful living.

3. Exegetical Observations
- Promise and response paired
- Urgency without fear

4. Scripture Interpreting Scripture

Titus 2:13

5. Christ-Centered Focus

Christ is both promise-giver and fulfillment.

6. Adventist Theological Trajectory

Second Coming hope

7. Sermon Movement

Promise → Response → Expectation

8. Pastoral Application

Live with readiness and hope.

9. Prayer and the Holy Spirit

Expectation and perseverance.

10. Training Notes

Avoid escapist language.

SERMON 48

A Call to Revival
Joel 2:12–13 (ESV)
Personal Bible Study
(Before Sermon Preparation)

Primary Scripture (ESV)

Joel 2:12–13

1. Read the Passage Slowly

- Observe God's invitation
- Note emphasis on the heart

2. Observe What the Text Says

- God calls for repentance
- Inner transformation matters more than outward display

3. Identify the Central Truth

God desires genuine repentance and restored hearts.

4. Let Scripture Interpret Scripture

Psalm 51:16–17; Isaiah 57:15

5. Personal Reflection Before God

- Is my repentance inward or external?
- Where is God calling me to return?

Prayer Before Moving Forward

Ask God for a renewed heart.

Sermon Training Outline
(For Public Teaching)

1. Primary Biblical Text

Joel 2:12–13 in prophetic appeal

2. Big Idea of the Text

True revival begins with heartfelt repentance.

3. Exegetical Observations
- "Return" implies restored relationship
- God's character invites repentance

4. Scripture Interpreting Scripture

Psalm 51:17

5. Christ-Centered Focus

Christ enables true repentance.

6. Adventist Theological Trajectory

Revival before restoration

7. Sermon Movement

Call → Response → Renewal

8. Pastoral Application

Respond sincerely to God's call.

9. Prayer and the Holy Spirit

Humility and renewal.

10. Training Notes

Avoid emotional manipulation.

SERMON 49

Preparing for the Coming King
Matthew 24:42–44 (ESV)
Personal Bible Study
(Before Sermon Preparation)

Primary Scripture (ESV)
Matthew 24:42–44

1. Read the Passage Slowly
- Observe the repeated call to watchfulness

2. Observe What the Text Says
- Timing is unknown
- Readiness is required

3. Identify the Central Truth
Faithful readiness marks true discipleship.

4. Let Scripture Interpret Scripture
Luke 12:35–40; 1 Thessalonians 5:6

5. Personal Reflection Before God
- What does readiness look like in my life?

Prayer Before Moving Forward
Ask God for watchful faithfulness.

Sermon Training Outline
(For Public Teaching)

1. Primary Biblical Text

Matthew 24:42–44 in eschatological teaching

2. Big Idea of the Text

Christ calls His followers to constant readiness.

3. Exegetical Observations

- Vigilance emphasized over calculation

4. Scripture Interpreting Scripture

1 Thessalonians 5:6

5. Christ-Centered Focus

Christ is the coming King.

6. Adventist Theological Trajectory

Advent readiness

7. Sermon Movement

Uncertainty → Readiness → Faithfulness

8. Pastoral Application

Live alert and faithful.

9. Prayer and the Holy Spirit

Watchfulness and trust.

10. Training Notes

Reject date-setting.

SERMON 50

Standing Firm in Truth
Ephesians 6:13 (ESV)
Personal Bible Study
(Before Sermon Preparation)

Primary Scripture (ESV)

Ephesians 6:13

1. Read the Passage Slowly

- Observe the call to stand
- Note preparation language

2. Observe What the Text Says

- Spiritual opposition is assumed
- God provides what is needed

3. Identify the Central Truth

God equips His people to stand firm in truth.

4. Let Scripture Interpret Scripture

Ephesians 6:10–18; John 17:17

5. Personal Reflection Before God

- Where am I tempted to compromise?

Prayer Before Moving Forward

Ask God for strength and stability.

Sermon Training Outline
(For Public Teaching)

1. Primary Biblical Text
Ephesians 6:13

2. Big Idea of the Text
God enables His people to stand firm.

3. Exegetical Observations
- Standing repeated for emphasis

4. Scripture Interpreting Scripture
John 17:17

5. Christ-Centered Focus
Christ is the truth believers stand in.

6. Adventist Theological Trajectory
End-time faithfulness

7. Sermon Movement
Opposition → Provision → Endurance

8. Pastoral Application
Stand faithfully in God's truth.

9. Prayer and the Holy Spirit
Strength and courage.

10. Training Notes
Avoid combative tone.

SERMON 51

The Patience of the Saints
Revelation 14:12 (ESV)
Personal Bible Study
(Before Sermon Preparation)

Primary Scripture (ESV)

Revelation 14:12

1. Read the Passage Slowly

- Observe characteristics of the saints

2. Observe What the Text Says

- Endurance defined
- Obedience and faith united

3. Identify the Central Truth

God's people endure through faithful obedience and trust.

4. Let Scripture Interpret Scripture

Hebrews 10:36; James 5:7–8

5. Personal Reflection Before God

- Where is patience required?

Prayer Before Moving Forward

Ask God for endurance.

Sermon Training Outline
(For Public Teaching)

1. Primary Biblical Text
Revelation 14:12

2. Big Idea of the Text
Faithful endurance marks God's people.

3. Exegetical Observations
- Patience linked with obedience

4. Scripture Interpreting Scripture
Hebrews 10:36

5. Christ-Centered Focus
Christ sustains endurance.

6. Adventist Theological Trajectory
End-time character

7. Sermon Movement
Pressure → Endurance → Faithfulness

8. Pastoral Application
Remain faithful under trial.

9. Prayer and the Holy Spirit
Perseverance and hope.

10. Training Notes
Avoid self-reliance.

SERMON 52

Finish the Work
Matthew 24:14 (ESV)
Personal Bible Study
(Before Sermon Preparation)

Primary Scripture (ESV)
Matthew 24:14

1. Read the Passage Slowly
- Observe gospel proclamation
- Note global scope

2. Observe What the Text Says
- Gospel must be proclaimed
- Christ's return follows

3. Identify the Central Truth
God's mission will be completed through faithful witness.

4. Let Scripture Interpret Scripture
Revelation 14:6; Acts 1:8

5. Personal Reflection Before God
- How do I participate in God's mission?

Prayer Before Moving Forward
Commit to faithful witness.

Sermon Training Outline

1. Primary Biblical Text
Matthew 24:14

2. Big Idea of the Text
The gospel will be proclaimed to all nations.

3. Exegetical Observations
- Mission precedes the end

4. Scripture Interpreting Scripture
Acts 1:8

5. Christ-Centered Focus
Christ commissions His church.

6. Adventist Theological Trajectory
Mission and urgency

7. Sermon Movement
Commission → Proclamation → Consummation

8. Pastoral Application
Participate faithfully in God's work.

9. Prayer and the Holy Spirit
Dependence and courage.

10. Training Notes
Emphasize faithfulness, not results.

Appendix A
How to Use This Book in the Local Church

This book was written to be used, not admired.

It is not a curriculum that must be followed in order, nor a collection of sermons to be repeated word for word. It is a training resource designed to help elders, lay leaders, teachers, and preachers grow in their confidence and faithfulness to Scripture over time.

Each unit begins with prayer and personal Bible study because the work of ministry always begins there. Scripture is meant to shape the servant before it is shared with others. If a chapter never becomes a sermon, the study has still accomplished its purpose.

In some contexts, lay leaders may even gather to work through the Personal Bible Study steps together before any sermon is preached, turning the study process itself into a training moment for the congregation. If a personal Bible study never becomes public teaching, it has still formed leaders and deepened the church.

For some, this book may be used in personal devotion and preparation. For others, it may support Sabbath

School teaching, small group leadership, or Bible study facilitation. In some churches, it may assist elders who preach regularly. In others, it may simply help leaders remain grounded in Scripture during seasons of transition or limited pastoral presence.

The sermon outlines included are intentionally incomplete. They are foundations, not finished products. They are meant to be adapted carefully, prayed over, and shaped by the local context and the leading of the Holy Spirit. Illustrations, personal stories, and specific applications should arise from the life of the congregation and the experience of the preacher.

This book assumes a willingness to do the work of study, prayer, and reflection. It is written for those who take seriously the responsibility of opening the Word of God before others. It may feel slow at times. That is intentional. Faithful ministry is not rushed.

Use this book as a companion, not a substitute. Let Scripture remain central. Let prayer remain primary. Let the Holy Spirit remain the true Teacher.

Appendix B
Recommended Study Tools and Resources

The tools used in Bible study are meant to serve the Word, not replace it.

Throughout this book, emphasis has been placed on careful observation, context, and allowing Scripture to interpret Scripture. The following resources are recommended because they support those goals without encouraging dependence on technical expertise or academic complexity.

A reliable Bible translation is essential. Scripture quotations in this book are taken from the English Standard Version (ESV) because of its close adherence to the original languages and suitability for careful study. Readers are encouraged to compare translations when helpful, always returning to the text itself.

A concordance is one of the most valuable tools available to lay leaders. It allows repeated words and themes to be traced through Scripture without speculation or guesswork. Cross-references, when used responsibly, help Scripture explain itself.

A basic Bible dictionary or handbook can provide helpful historical and cultural background, particularly when studying unfamiliar settings or customs. These should be used to illuminate the text, not to override it.

For word studies, restraint is important. Not every word requires analysis, and meanings should never be forced. When used, language tools should confirm what the context already suggests, not introduce new ideas.

Notebooks, journals, or digital notes are strongly encouraged. Writing slows the mind and helps clarify thought. Over time, patterns of study, questions, and insights become visible and form a personal library of reflection.

Above all, prayer remains the most essential resource. No tool can replace humility before the Word or dependence on the Spirit of God. Preparation without prayer may produce information, but it will not produce transformation.

Recommended Online Study Platforms (2026)

Digital tools can support careful study when they are used to illuminate the text rather than replace engagement with it. The following resources are widely available and can help elders and lay leaders practice the disciplines described in this book while keeping Scripture central.

Logos Bible Software offers an extensive digital library, original-language tools, and sermon preparation features. It is most useful for pastors, Bible workers, and lay leaders committed to long-term, in-depth study.

Bible Gateway provides a simple way to read and compare multiple translations, listen to audio Bibles, and search for passages quickly. It is especially helpful for public reading and basic preparation.

Bible Hub collects side-by-side translations, interlinear Greek and Hebrew, commentaries, and lexical tools. It is best used to check and deepen observations that first arise from personal reading.

Blue Letter Bible makes Strong's Concordance, word-study tools, and cross-references easily accessible. It serves lay leaders who want to begin responsible word studies without relying on advanced software.

YouVersion offers reading plans, audio options, and simple ways to share Scripture. It is particularly effective for daily devotion, group plans, and encouraging congregational engagement with the Bible.

STEP Bible allows detailed exploration of original languages and cross-text connections at no cost. It is well suited for leaders who wish to trace themes and words across Scripture in greater depth.

BibleProject provides videos, podcasts, and reading guides that explain biblical books, themes, and literary structures. These resources can help visual learners and enrich group study and preaching preparation.

Olive Tree Bible Software is a clean, mobile-friendly app with strong offline capabilities. It is especially valuable for leaders who travel or serve in remote areas with limited internet access.

e-Sword is a classic offline Bible study program with downloadable translations and commentaries, particularly useful where connectivity is unreliable.

These tools should follow, not replace, slow reading, observation, and prayer. They serve best when they confirm what the text already shows rather than when they are used as shortcuts to avoid the hard work of listening to Scripture.

Appendix C
A Prayer for Elders and Lay Leaders

Lord,

You have entrusted Your Word to ordinary people and asked them to handle it with care. We confess that this responsibility is greater than our ability and heavier than our strength.

Teach us to approach Scripture with humility. Guard us from using Your Word carelessly or speaking where we have not first listened. Keep us from the temptation to perform rather than to serve.

Give us patience in study and faithfulness in preparation. Help us to value understanding more than speed, truth more than approval, and obedience more than recognition.

When we teach or preach, let Your Spirit lead. When we visit, let Your presence go before us. When we are unsure, teach us to wait. When we are weary, remind us that this work is Yours.

Shape us into leaders who love Scripture, love people, and remain teachable. May our service strengthen Your church and point others to the hope we have in Christ.

We place this work in Your hands and ask that You guide it according to Your will.

Amen.

Selected Bibliography

Andrews, J. N. *The History of the Sabbath and the First Day of the Week.* Battle Creek, MI: Review and Herald Publishing Association, 1873.

Bates, Joseph. *The Seventh Day Sabbath, a Perpetual Sign.* New Bedford, MA: Benjamin Lindsey, 1846.

Knight, George R. *A Brief History of Seventh-day Adventists.* Hagerstown, MD: Review and Herald Publishing Association, 2012.

Knight, George R. *Millennial Fever and the End of the World.* Boise, ID: Pacific Press Publishing Association, 1993.

Knight, George R. *Reading Ellen White: How to Understand and Apply Her Writings.* Hagerstown, MD: Review and Herald Publishing Association, 1997.

Knight, George R. *The Apocalyptic Vision and the Neutering of Adventism.* Hagerstown, MD: Review and Herald Publishing Association, 2008.

McArthur, Benjamin L. "J. N. Andrews: The First Missionary." *Adventist Heritage* 4, no. 1 (1977): 12–18.

Miller, William. *Evidence from Scripture and History of the Second Coming of Christ.* Boston: Joshua V. Himes, 1842.

Ministerial Association, General Conference of Seventh-day Adventists. *Elder's Manual.* Silver Spring, MD: General Conference of Seventh-day Adventists, 2010.

Nichol, F. D. *The Midnight Cry: A Defense of the Character and Conduct of William Miller*. Washington, DC: Review and Herald Publishing Association, 1944.

Seventh-day Adventist Church. *Church Manual*. 21st ed., rev. 2025. Silver Spring, MD: General Conference of Seventh-day Adventists, 2025.

Valentine, Gilbert M. *The Shaping of Adventism: The Case of W. C. White and the Ellen G. White Estate*. Berrien Springs, MI: Andrews University Press, 1992.

Valentine, Gilbert. "John N. Andrews Symposium." *Adventist Heritage* 9, no. 1 (1984): 12.

White, Ellen G. *Counsels on Sabbath School Work*. Washington, DC: Review and Herald Publishing Association, 1913.

White, Ellen G. *Counsels to Parents, Teachers, and Students*. Mountain View, CA: Pacific Press Publishing Association, 1913.

White, Ellen G. *Education*. Mountain View, CA: Pacific Press Publishing Association, 1903.

White, Ellen G. *Evangelism*. Washington, DC: Review and Herald Publishing Association, 1946.

White, Ellen G. *Gospel Workers*. Washington, DC: Review and Herald Publishing Association, 1915.

White, Ellen G. *Life Sketches*. Mountain View, CA: Pacific Press Publishing Association, 1915.

White, Ellen G. *Selected Messages*. Book 1. Washington, DC: Review and Herald Publishing Association, 1958.

White, Ellen G. *Steps to Christ*. Mountain View, CA: Pacific Press Publishing Association, 1892.

White, Ellen G. *Testimonies for the Church*. Vol. 5. Mountain View, CA: Pacific Press Publishing Association, 1889.

White, Ellen G. *The Great Controversy*. Mountain View, CA: Pacific Press Publishing Association, 1911.

White, Ellen G. *The Ministry of Healing*. Mountain View, CA: Pacific Press Publishing Association, 1905.

About the Author

Michael A. Reahl has served as a lay leader in rural and military-adjacent contexts, including Alaska. He has formal training in biblical studies and languages and has worked closely with elders and lay leaders in small and under-resourced congregations. His ministry and writing emphasize Scripture-first study, careful observation, and Christ-centered teaching shaped by faithful engagement with the biblical text.

Advent Awareness Ministries LLC

Alaska

www.ingramcontent.com/pod-product-compliance
Lightning Source LLC
Chambersburg PA
CBHW051523150726
47997CB00001B/363